ST. PAUL'S CATHEDRAL AS IT APPEARED
DURING THE HEIGHT OF THE NAZI
FIRE RAID OF DECEMBER 29, 1940

Received From Daily Hearld
1/12/41

John Livendale
13 Main St North
Coaltown of Wemyr
Fife

THE WAR
IN PICTURES

SECOND YEAR

ODHAMS PRESS LIMITED

LONG ACRE, LONDON, W.C. 2

" Never in the field of human conflict was so much owed by so many to so few."

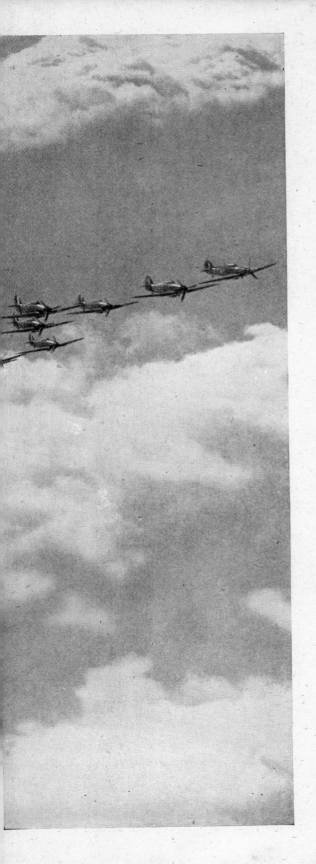

BRITAIN AT BAY

O N 3 SEPTEMBER, 1940, Britain had been at war with Germany for one year. The enemy, employing blitzkrieg tactics, had overrun six countries; Poland, Denmark, Norway, Holland, Belgium and France had in turn succumbed, and Britain's armies, driven back to the sea, had only escaped from Continental soil by a miracle. Small wonder that the Germans boasted that the war would be over by the end of 1940, that their Fuehrer would enter London in triumph before Christmas.

The collapse of all Continental resistance gave the enemy complete command of Europe's western seaboard from Narvik in the north to the Spanish frontier in the south. It gave him air and naval bases on the very doorstep of Britain, the coasts of which were now within easy range of his guns.

But if Germany was to win the war before the end of the year an invasion of Britain was necessary. This could only be attempted after crippling or destroying her fleet and driving her air force from the skies.

To achieve this end Hitler relied upon his air force, the Luftwaffe, and plans were drawn up during June, July and the first week in August for what was to have been the final attack. By 8 August the enemy was ready, and on that day he launched massed formations of dive bombers, powerfully escorted by fighters, on British convoys in the neighbourhood of Bournemouth and the Isle of Wight. His airmen were soon to learn that this was to be no easy victory, that the calibre of the British fighter pilots was greater than their own and that the eight-gun " Spitfires " and " Hurricanes " were more than a match for Germany's much-vaunted Messerschmitt and Heinkel fighters.

By 12 August German losses had amounted to 182 planes, and the enemy began to realize that he had underestimated the strength of the opposition. If he was to achieve his purpose British fighters must be destroyed on the ground. So, whilst still maintaining his attacks on shipping and coastal towns, he sent large forces to attack fighter stations in south and south-east England. Again the pilots of the R.A.F. were equal to the

3

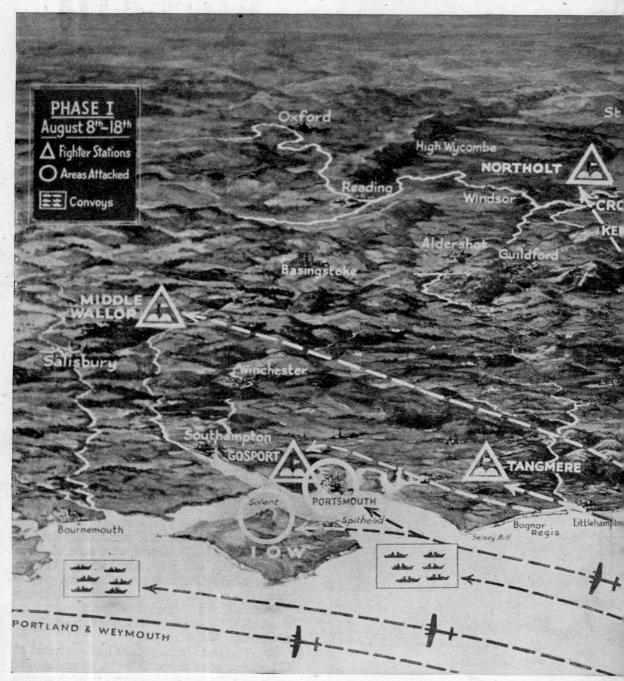

PHASE I
August 8th-18th
△ Fighter Stations
○ Areas Attacked
▦ Convoys

Oxford

High Wycombe

NORTHOLT

Reading

Windsor

CR...

KE...

Aldershot

Guildford

Basingstoke

MIDDLE
WALLOP

Salisbury

Winchester

Southampton

GOSPORT

TANGMERE

Bournemouth

Solent

PORTSMOUTH

Spithead

Bognor
Regis

Littlehampton

Selsey Bill

I.O.W.

St

PORTLAND & WEYMOUTH

BEGINNING OF THE AIR OFFENSIVE. On 8 August, Germany decided that the time had come to launch the carefully prepared air attack on Britain which was to prelude an invasion of her shores. Her principal need—to establish full mastery of the air—was to be secured by putting fighter airfields out of action, thus keeping the R.A.F. to the ground. As a first step massed bomber formations, escorted by fighters, attacked Channel convoys and coastal towns. These attacks soon showed that British fighter strength was greater and more formidable than had been anticipated, for in the first five days 182 German planes were destroyed. On 15, 16 and 18 August heavy attacks were launched against fighter aerodromes between London and the

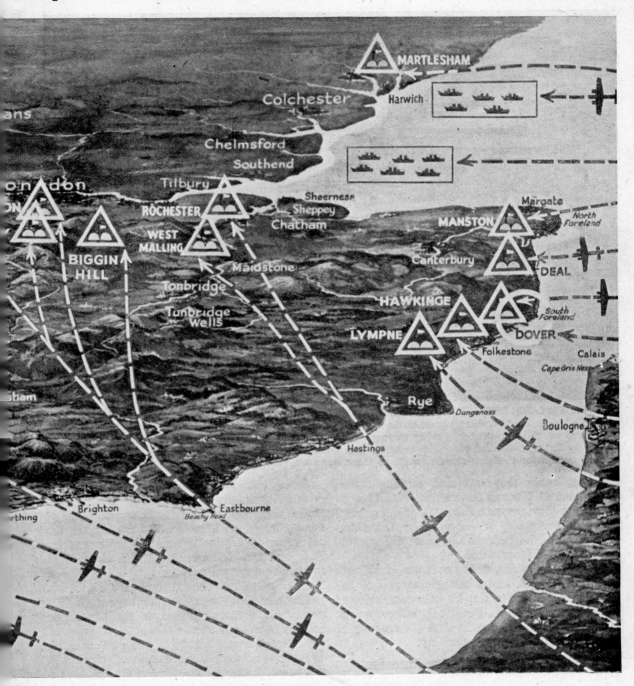

coast—the above map, reproduced from the Ministry of Information booklet, "The Battle of Britain," shows the direction and objectives of the attacks, which cost Germany 435 planes. The tactics usually adopted by the Luftwaffe was to begin an attack by bombing coastal objectives, in an attempt to draw off British fighters while making the main assault on its real objective, whether aerodrome or port, about half an hour later. In the ten days—8 to 18 August—of this first phase of the Battle of Britain, the total German losses amounted to 697 aircraft against a British loss of 153 machines, sixty of whose pilots were safe. An even greater proportion of British pilots would have been saved, had not so much of the fighting taken place over the sea.

Nazi raiders leave their mark in the sky September, 1940

DOG FIGHT OVER THE CITY OF LONDON. During the later months of 1940, when the Battle of Britain was at its height, Nazi bombing planes made repeated attempts to penetrate the capital's defences. The small formations which succeeded in getting through were hotly engaged by British fighters, but so high did the enemy fly that no indication of the fierce battles that were going on overhead was visible to watchers on the ground except for feathery streaks, such as those seen above, which the combatants left in their wake.

occasion, again they met and outfought the tightly-packed German formations. On 15 and 16 August they accounted for 245 of the enemy and by 18 August, ten days after the start of the battle, the Luftwaffe had lost 697 planes against a British loss of 153.

Even the Luftwaffe, strong as it was, could not stand such losses, and Goering was obliged to call a halt in order to rest his pilots and reform his depleted squadrons. For five days there was a lull in the battle, but on the sixth (24 August) it was rejoined with even greater fury.

ATTACKS ON INLAND AERODROMES

It soon became evident that the Germans were employing new tactics, for instead of concentrating on coastal aerodromes, fighter stations farther inland became their main objectives. The method of attack, too, was altered, the number of bombers being materially reduced and the fighter escorts almost doubled.

Again Britain's fighters took grim toll of the raiders; again the enemy failed to dent the British defences. During this, the second phase of the battle, which lasted until 5 September, the enemy had launched thirty-five main attacks. They cost him 562 aircraft. British losses were small in comparison, amounting to 219 machines. Goering was again obliged to change his tactics.

The third phase began on 7 September. On that memorable Saturday afternoon the sun shone brightly in a cloudless sky. Suddenly the peace of the afternoon was broken by the wail of sirens and soon the distant drone of approaching aircraft was heard. It was the vanguard of Goering's warplanes approaching the capital in what turned out to be the first raid of the third phase of the Battle of Britain—the mass attacks on London.

The enemy approached in several waves, each composed of formations of between twenty and forty bombers escorted by an equal number of fighters. In all, some 350 machines crossed the coast, and although hotly engaged by British fighters over Kent and Surrey many succeeded in breaking through and inflicting considerable damage on the dockland areas. Dogfights took place over the capital itself and many Londoners had the thrilling experience of seeing enemy planes diving earthwards, smoke pouring from their engines. During this raid the enemy lost 103 aircraft.

When night fell clouds of smoke that had been seen rising from the direction of the docks assumed a sinister reddish tinge and throughout the hours of darkness the enemy followed up his advantage by dropping high explosive bombs into the heart of the fires he had started. It was a night of horror for London's firemen and the East End A.R.P. services. Altogether in that first great London raid the casualties amounted to 306 killed and 1,337 wounded.

Despite its enormous losses the Luftwaffe continued to press home its daylight attacks on the capital with great tenacity and daring. Many of

these failed to pierce the fighter and anti-aircraft defences, but on 11 September about thirty aircraft succeeded in reaching London and unloading their bombs. The raiding force again lost heavily, ninety planes being shot down.

THE GREATEST DAY

The climax of the battle was reached on Sunday the 15th when 500 German aircraft, 250 in the morning and 250 in the afternoon, made their most determined assault on London. They were met and hotly engaged over the Channel by "Hurricanes" and "Spitfires," but again many raiders succeeded in penetrating the defences by sheer weight of numbers. During this attack bombs damaged many buildings, but the total damage done was small in comparison with the shattering defeat inflicted upon the enemy. No fewer than 185 of their machines were destroyed in actions that were described by the Prime Minister as "the most brilliant and fruitful of any fought upon a large scale up to date by

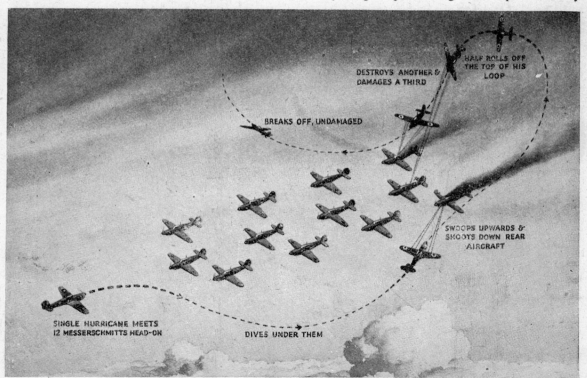

"HURRICANE" TAKES ON TWELVE MESSERSCHMITTS. The Luftwaffe, while possessing every advantage of superior numbers in the Battle of Britain, was frequently nonplussed by the skill and daring of the British fighter pilots. Many encounters took place in which disproportionately greater enemy forces failed to make use of their numerical advantage. In one such exploit a single "Hurricane," meeting a formation of twelve Messerschmitts, destroyed two and damaged a third before its pilot, his own machine still undamaged, broke off the action. The picture, reproduced from "The Battle of Britain," shows the tactics of the British pilot.

London sleeps underground

" SAFETY FIRST " GETS A NEW MEANING. When the night raids began in earnest, London's Tubes became improvised shelters for tens of thousands of civilians, especially women and children, who settled down with their bedding each night on the platforms, as seen in the above picture. After the first few weeks, however, bunks were installed (below) and other arrangements for the comfort of the shelterers were made.

fighters of the Royal Air Force." It was the greatest day in the Battle of Britain.

Despite this crushing reverse German bombers continued their daylight attacks on the capital until 5 October. During this period there were three major assaults made, 27 September, 30 September and 5 October. The German losses of 205 planes were again out of all proportion to the results achieved.

By this time it must have become apparent to the German High Command that such raids were unavailing, for bombers that succeeded in reaching the capital were so promptly tackled and so severely handled by British fighters that accurate

damage. In addition, the enemy pilots showed little inclination to meet the British fighters who had achieved a moral ascendancy. Whenever they met a British fighter they jettisoned their bombs and made off. These tip-and-run raids continued until the end of October, when they gradually died away.

PREMIER'S TRIBUTE TO R.A.F.

Thus ended this vital phase of the Battle of Britain. It was won by a handful of young men who cheerfully faced death not once, but many times a day, who met and outfought a numerically superior enemy force high in the sky above their

HOSPITALS SUFFER IN THE NIGHT RAIDS. Many of London's hospitals suffered severe damage from the Nazi bombs, yet casualties among the patients were remarkably few. This was due in large measure to the bravery of the hospital staffs who carried on with their work calmly, however fierce the bombardment, always putting the comfort of their patients before their own safety. The picture shows damage done by blast to the ward of a London hospital. Nurses and students are searching for such equipment as can be salved.

bombing was impossible. In addition, the heavy losses must have adversely affected the morale of the attacking force.

Nevertheless, the enemy did not entirely give up the fight. Instead he changed his tactics for a third time. He withdrew nearly all his bombers and used only fighters and fighter-bombers, mostly Messerschmitt "109's" and "110's." Although his losses diminished, the bomb load of these planes was not sufficient to do any real

native land. Between 8 August and 31 October they destroyed 2,375 enemy planes. The victory was not achieved without loss. The R.A.F. lost 375 pilots killed and 358 wounded.

The Prime Minister himself expressed the feelings of the nation when he said: "The gratitude of every home in our island, in our Empire, and indeed throughout the world, except in the abodes of the guilty, goes out to the British airmen who, undaunted by odds, unwearied in their constant

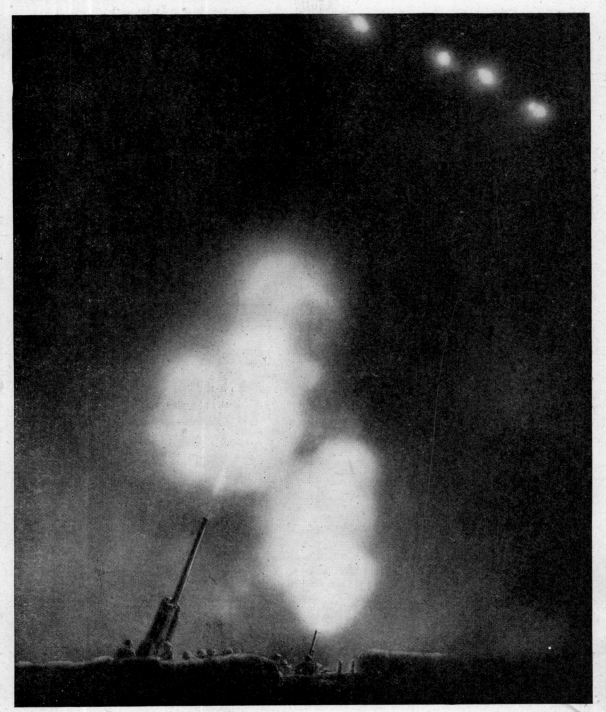

A.A. GUNNERS EXTINGUISH ENEMY FLARES. The night raiders frequently dropped parachute flares in order to illuminate the ground, thus making the identification of their targets possible. The flares which burnt for several minutes and descended very slowly, also enabled night reconnaissance planes to photograph the results achieved by bombs already dropped. It was the duty of the A.A. gunners to shoot these out before they could be useful to the raiders. Above, a battery is firing at a line of flares that have just been dropped.

Firemen tackle a city blaze

DOUGHTY WORK OF THE FIRE-FIGHTERS. London's fire services had been increased more than tenfold in personnel and equipment, and the firemen, both regulars and auxiliary, worked at full pressure to combat the effects of the high explosive and incendiary bombs that were showered night after night on the capital. Thanks to the heroism of these men, many of whom lost their lives, the fires started by the enemy rarely got out of control, for the firemen were on the spot so quickly that the flames had little time to get a hold.

AFTER THE RAIDERS HAD GONE. Although Germany's daylight raiders met with small success in their attacks on London, those that came by night succeeded in causing considerable damage to property, besides killing and injuring many civilians. This view of the approach to London Bridge is a typical example of the scenes of devastation that greeted city workers on their way to their offices the morning after a raid.

PUBLIC SERVICES CARRY ON. Often the Londoner on his way to the office after a night raid on the capital found pipes and cables severed, and traffic turned aside, by bomb-craters such as that in the Strand seen above. But skilled repair squads soon had such matters in hand, and it was seldom indeed that the Nazi bombers succeeded in dislocating public services in any locality for more than two or three days.

challenge and mortal danger, are turning the tide of the world by their prowess and by their devotion. Never in the field of human conflict was so much owed by so many to so few."

Whilst the Luftwaffe was carrying out the first stage of Germany's invasion plan, preparations were being pressed forward for the main assault by land and sea. Picked troops were concentrating on the other side of the Channel and the barges and ships that were to carry them to Britain were being fitted out in readiness for Der Tag.

Against these troop and barge concentrations the bomber planes of the Bomber and Coastal Commands were constantly operating. Night after night, in all kinds of weather, they crossed the Channel and pounded the invasion bases with tons of high explosive and incendiary bombs.

They made it impossible for the barges and other vessels to remain in one place for any length of time and forced them to move from port to port in a vain effort to elude detection.

In addition to these operations, long-range bombers penetrated deep into enemy territory in an effort to slow down the German industrial machine and hamper communications. Munition factories, oil plants, canals, railways and marshalling yards were special targets for British bombers which had to fly across hundreds of miles of enemy territory to reach their objectives.

The best tribute to the success of these operations was paid by Hitler himself who, in a speech on 4 September, threatened dreadful reprisals if the British did not cease "the nuisance of nightly and planless bomb throwing." Britain's answer was to bomb the industrial areas of Berlin and

RESCUE SQUAD AT WORK. During the long lull before serious air attacks developed, demolition and rescue workers had been intensively trained to deal with whatever might await them. The call, when it came, found them ready. The picture shows a party rescuing a victim from the ruins of a bombed building.

penetrate as far east as Stettin, in Pomerania, on the following night.

Thus, by raiding enemy sources of supply, disorganizing his road, rail and canal traffic and bombing his troops and ships marshalled for invasion, the bomber pilots kept the enemy at arm's length whilst the Fighter Command broke his attempts to gain air supremacy.

During these anxious autumn days when the people of Britain watched and waited for the invader, Britain's armies were not idle. The coast of Britain assumed the aspect of a battle-field; barbed wire and guns commanded every likely line of approach. Troops trained constantly in the art of mechanized warfare and carried out extensive manœuvres in readiness for the day when the enemy should come.

Meanwhile Britain's civilian army, the Home Guard, watched all approaches to the chief cities and towns. They built pillboxes and dug trenches during the warm evenings of late summer for, like their professional comrades, they were determined to give a good account of themselves.

But the invader did not come. His failure to defeat the R.A.F. or to drive the Navy from the seas made the project too hazardous even for Hitler. Instead he sent his bombers over by night in a gigantic attempt to break down civilian morale and win the war by a campaign of terror.

NIGHT RAIDS ON LONDON

The first large-scale night raid on London, as already described, followed the daylight bombing of the London docks on 7-8 September. The next night the raiders came again. The sirens announced their arrival at dusk and their departure at dawn the following morning. During these nine hours bombs fell on many parts of the

Homeless victims of the Nazi bombs

HITLER'S SHADOW OVER EAST LONDON. The realities of the Nazi "new world order" were vividly brought home to the poorer parts of London and other industrial towns by the German air terror campaign. Many an East London mother, like this one weeping with her two babies on a doorstep, her every possession destroyed, might be seen in those September days sitting, in tears, near the ruins of her bombed home.

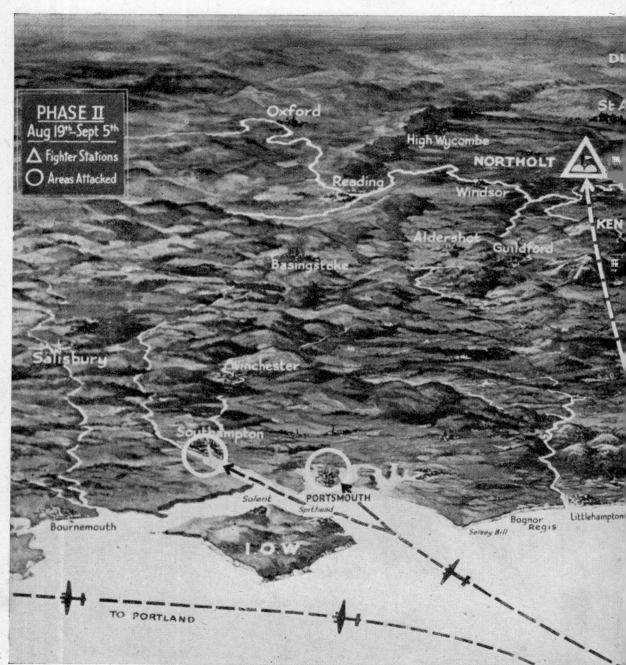

LUFTWAFFE'S ATTACKS ON FIGHTER BASES. A short lull of five days, filled by reconnaissance flights in which thirty-nine German planes were shot down, separated the second phase of the Battle of Britain from the first. From 24 August to 5 September the main weight of the German attack was directed against fighter aerodromes and aircraft factories inland. During the first six days of this phase heavy attacks were directed on Portland, Southampton, Portsmouth, Dover and Folkestone, areas in Kent and Essex, and the Thames Estuary; on 30 August and the succeeding days the aerodromes on the London outskirts and in Kent were the chief objectives. Although damage was done to the airfields attacked, the attempt to put the British fighter squadrons out of action was a complete failure; and, whether from a determination to stick to a prearranged

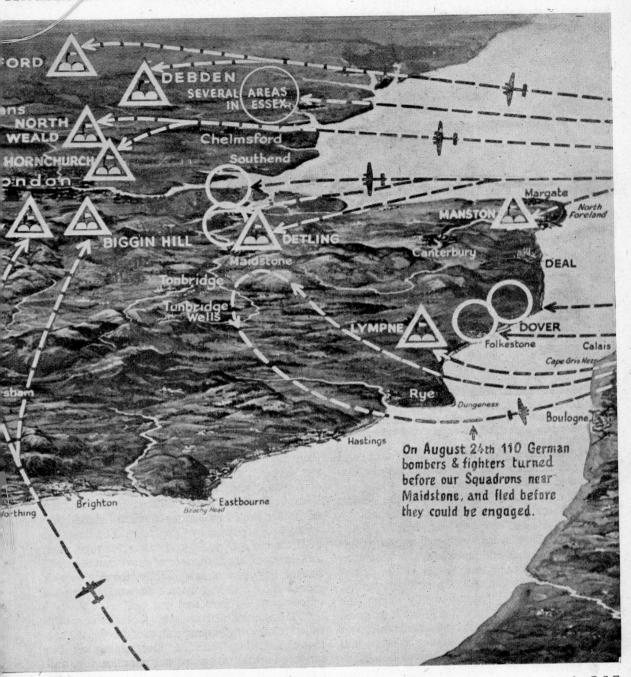

On August 24th 110 German bombers & fighters turned before our Squadrons near Maidstone, and fled before they could be engaged.

time-table, or because it was wrongly supposed that sufficient damage had been done to make the R.A.F. incapable of defending London, this phase of the struggle was closed on 5 September. Thirty-five main attacks were made during this stage of the battle; they resulted in a loss of 562 German bombers and fighters: probably hundreds more shared their fate, for the official score included only cases of certain destruction. British losses were 219 aircraft; but the pilots of these were saved in 132 cases. The objectives of this stage are shown in the map above, reproduced from the Ministry of Information booklet, "The Battle of Britain." It was carried through with smaller bomber formations than those previously employed, with larger fighter escorts, the latter flying partly at great height, partly in box formation round and slightly above the bombers.

HOW LONDON ANSWERED THE BLITZ. The morning after a raid, London's housewives came out as usual to do their shopping amidst the debris. Their oranges tasted none the worse for the knowledge that they had come unscathed through that Mediterranean which Hitler's Italian ally claimed for his private sea.

capital, interfering with public services and causing considerable damage to property besides killing and injuring 1,800 people.

During the nights that followed the raiders visited the capital with monotonous regularity. Damage to life and property was great and many famous buildings were damaged, among them numerous hospitals and churches. Yet the enemy had failed to damage the morale of the British people or to shake their faith in ultimate victory.

Britain's civilians behaved calmly during the heaviest raids, and her A.R.P. services functioned perfectly from the start. Firemen, wardens, rescue and demolition parties and others behaved like seasoned troops in face of the fiercest bombardments from the air, and more than justified the long months of training they had undergone. The heroic work of these brave men and women did much to lessen the effect of the German bombs and to keep the vital services of the country intact. Their courage and devotion to duty did not go unrecognized.

As early as September the King paid tribute to their bravery and devotion when he instituted the George Cross. In announcing this new decoration, which ranked second only to the Victoria Cross, he said: "To the men and women of the Air Raid Precautions Services I should like to say a special word of gratitude. The devotion of these civilian workers, firemen, salvage men, and many others in the face of grave and constant danger has won a new renown for the British name. These men and women are worthy partners of our armed forces and our police . . .

"The men and women in the factories or on the railways who work on regardless of danger, though the sirens have sounded, maintaining all the services and necessities of our common life, and keeping the fighting line well supplied with weapons, earn their place among the heroes of this war. No less honour is due to all those who, night after night, endure discomfort, hardship and peril in their homes and shelters . . .

"The walls of London may be battered, but the spirit of the Londoner stands resolute and undismayed."

CITY WORKERS WATCH BATTLE IN THE SKY. On 6 September, London had six daylight alerts lasting with only short intervals from dawn to dusk. Waves of attacking planes that flew in over the Thames Estuary were hotly engaged by London's fighter defences which succeeded in destroying forty-six during the day. Again and again Londoners' eyes turned skywards to watch the trails of the combatants high above the city.

ABDICATION OF KING CAROL. Unrest in Rumania had grown rapidly since her government, in June, ceded Bessarabia and Northern Bukovina, with a combined population of about four millions, to the U.S.S.R. In August, Nazi pressure had forced her to give up Southern Dobruja to Bulgaria, and, a week later, to restore to Hungary about two-thirds of Transylvania, annexed after the last war. Widespread rioting, in which the Fascist Iron Guard played a prominent part, took place all over the country, and on the morning of 6 September King Carol abdicated in favour of his eighteen-year-old son Michael. The Premier, General Antonescu, who assumed dictatorial powers as Conductor or Leader, is seen (above) addressing a meeting, with a small group of green-shirted Iron Guards standing to attention below. Next to him stands the Iron Guard leader, Horea Sima. The portrait above the dais is that of Codreanu, the former Iron Guard leader, shot "while attempting to escape" when under arrest for causing an uprising against the former regime. Below, Iron Guard legionaries, side by side with men in native dress, are marching through a square in Bucharest.

U.S. destroyers transferred to Britain

NAVAL AID FROM AMERICA. The first batch of the fifty destroyers handed over to Britain by agreement with the U.S.A. arrived at a Canadian port on 7 September. Above, American and Canadian sailors fraternize on the deck of one of the ships; below, Canadian officers and ratings march to take over one of the new vessels.

AIR ATTACK ON EAST LONDON

7 SEPTEMBER, 1940

The full fury of the Nazi attempt to destroy London from the air was loosed on 7 September in a twelve-hour day and night raid. In the biggest attack on the capital so far made, two forces of enemy planes, totalling about 400 in number, flew up the Thames Estuary towards London. Many of them succeeded in penetrating its defences, and unloading their bombs on the industrial and waterside areas on both sides of the river east of the city. Many bombs fell on the docks, setting fire to barges and warehouses; as the attack developed it became more indiscriminate, bombs falling at random on churches, schools, shops, and hundreds of working-class homes. In spite of the heroic work of the civil defence services, several great fires raged for many hours, and some 400 people were killed and 1,500 injured. One hundred and three enemy planes, about a quarter of the raiding force, were shot down by the R.A.F., which itself lost twenty-two fighter planes. The drawing by Feliks Topolski, specially made for this book and reproduced here, gives a vivid impression of the scenes of horror in London's East End as Goering's messengers of death hovered over the capital.

Germans set Dockland ablaze

DOCKLAND RAID THROUGH GERMAN EYES. Long before the war, the Germans had claimed that, if they wished, they could in a few hours reduce the whole of East London's docks and riverside areas to a heap of blazing rubble. On 7 September, with a force of about 400 bombers, they did their best to carry out their threat. Their own official photographs, one of which is seen above, show that the effects of the raids, serious as they were, fell very far short of their hopes. Thanks to the R.A.F., the attempt to treat London as Rotterdam had been served did not succeed—and its cost had been 114 German planes destroyed in two days.

U.S. tanks for Canadian Tank Corps

AMERICA'S MOUNTING AID. As the months passed, American public opinion became increasingly convinced that the freedom of the United States and the future of democracy depended upon the victory of the Allied cause. The wheels of American industry moved faster and faster, and, as war production got into its stride, the spate of supplies for the British forces continually rose. A train of whippet tanks, purchased by the Canadian Government for use at Canadian Tank Corps training grounds, is here seen arriving at Camp Borden, Canada. Some of them bore chalked messages from America, such as "Good luck, Canada—Take 'em away."

PREPARING FOR ATTACK ON ITALY'S EMPIRE. During the first phase of operations in the Western Desert, stated General Wavell, a small British mobile force had completely dominated the eastern frontier of Libya in face of greatly superior Italian forces, and full plans had been made to meet the enemy attack when it should come. Units of French Colonial infantry under General de Gaulle's banner were formed to share in the defence of Egypt. Meanwhile Britain's growing forces were heavily reinforced during September,

numerous detachments of land troops and airmen from Great Britain, India, Australia and New Zealand being disembarked at ports in the Middle East. The upper picture shows Indian troops lined up on the quayside after disembarking from a transport; below, left, a troopship coming alongside to discharge from its loaded decks hundreds of warriors eager to show the Duce that his claim to be lord of the Eastern Mediterranean is not by any means beyond dispute; right, airmen from Great Britain disembarking with their kit.

Berlin feels the blast of British bombs 10 September, 1940

HOW BRITAIN HIT BACK. The R.A.F. paid frequent visits to Berlin, often staying for several hours over the city, which contained many military objectives. On 10 September, said the Germans, the Reichstag and the garden of Goebbels's house were hit. Above, German Safety Service workers putting out a fire started by British incendiary bombs; below, civilians clearing away the debris after a night raid on Germany's capital.

RAIDER'S FEAT — AND RAIDER'S FATE. In the early morning of 10 September a delayed action bomb caused extensive damage at the King's London home.   Five days later another bomb hit the Palace.   Above their Majesties are seen inspecting the damage.   The shop outside Victoria Station (below) was demolished by a raider—believed to be the plane that bombed the Palace on the 15th—which fell on to it in flames.

SEPTEMBER 13, 1940: ITALIANS INVADE EGYPT. Mussolini's troops began their long-awaited advance into Egypt early in September, and on the 13th they crossed the frontier and occupied El Sollum. Here Italian troops are seen advancing across the desert under a covering barrage from their artillery.

Italian tanks and infantry

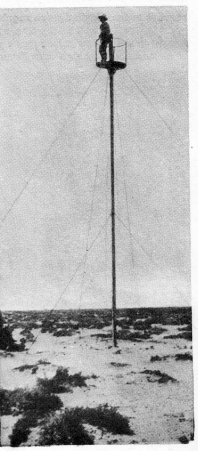

ITALY FACES BRITAIN ON EGYPTIAN SOIL. After occupying Sollum and the customs post of El Musaid on 13 September, the Italian forces, consisting of infantry, mechanized units, Blackshirt units and camel corps, penetrated a few miles further into the trackless and waterless desert by way of Wadi Halfaya, nicknamed by the British "Hellfire Pass." Artillery fire caused them heavy losses. The British deliberately withdrew before the Italian advance in order to tempt the enemy into a dangerous lengthening of their lines of communication. Meanwhile the Duce's troops were constantly harried by tanks and the R.A.F., and by the Fleet's guns from the sea. The pictures show: above, Italian soldiers supported by caterpillar-pulled artillery advancing near El Sollum; below, left, British tank crews "cleaning up" in the Western desert; centre, Italian machine gunners taking cover in shallow trenches near El Sollum; right, an Italian desert "spotter" looking out for the dreaded raiding parties of British tanks.

R.A.F. bomb German Channel guns

ATTACKS ON GERMAN COASTAL GUNS. The big German guns that bombarded Dover and British convoys in the Channel were regularly subjected to intense bombardment both by the R.A.F. and long-range guns on the British coast. The enemy emplacements were cunningly camouflaged and strongly guarded by anti-aircraft guns which put up a fierce barrage whenever British planes appeared (above). Below, bomb and shell damage in a French coastal town that was unfortunate enough to harbour a "Big Bertha."

THWARTING THE INVASION MENACE. Hitler's repeated threats to invade Britain remained threats as yet—thanks in large measure, no doubt, to the good work put in by British bombers. While their brothers of the Fighter Command battled against enemy raiders in the skies above Britain, they flew across to the French, Dutch and Belgian ports almost nightly to upset the results of the Germans' day's work. Special attention was paid to the troop-carrying barges which lay ready for a swoop on the English coast. This British official photograph shows the dock area at Dunkirk, where many of the invasion barges were concentrated, after a visit from the Royal Air Force. Damaged barges can be seen near the entrance to the upper dock; the warehouses surrounding it are completely destroyed, while two big buildings facing the other dock have been demolished and the centre one gutted by fire. The wharves, roads and sidings are pitted with bomb craters.

R.A.F. DISARRANGE HITLER'S ARMADA. The constant visits of British bombers to the "invasion ports" wrought havoc with the Fuehrer's preparations for a direct onslaught by sea on Britain, the enemy vessels slipping from port to port under cover of night in their unsuccessful efforts to find a safe harbourage. In day and night attacks, Le Havre, Antwerp, Calais, Ostend, Dunkirk, Zeebrugge and the islands off the Dutch coast were all visited in turn, many tons of high explosive and incendiary bombs being dropped on docks and

shipping, causing fires visible many miles away. Convoys and supply ships were special targets, and all the efforts of German fighter planes were insufficient to protect the massed shipping. Above is an impression, specially drawn by Charles Cundall, A.R.A., of a night raid on a Channel port. Darkness is turned into day by the blaze from burning barges and dockside buildings as the searchlights sweep the sky in ineffectual efforts to hold the British planes whose deadly accuracy of aim contrasts strangely with the Luftwaffe's indiscriminate fury.

SEPTEMBER, 1940 : "NAVY PATROLS "ITALIAN LAKE." Mussolini's boastful claim to the Mediterranean as an Italian preserve did not prevent British battleships, as the picture shows, from continuing to sweep its waters in search of the Duce's strangely shy navy. The triple torpedo-tube swung outboard for action shows that Britannia has not relinquished her rule of the waves.

British fighter pilots shoot down

BRITAIN'S AERIAL TRAFALGAR. 15 September marked the climax of the Battle of Britain. On that day 500 German aircraft, 250 in the morning and 250 in the afternoon, made a most determined attempt to reach London. "Spitfires" and "Hurricanes" that went up to intercept the enemy broke up the raiding formations and the battle developed into a series of running fights. By the end of the day the British pilots had accounted for 185 enemy machines, and unofficial estimates raised the Nazi loss to 232. British losses were twenty-five planes, thirteen of whose pilots were saved. The picture shows a "Hurricane" giving a victorious sweep over the relics of its victim, a Heinkel "111" bomber, shot down in one of the many encounters of the day.

GERMAN BOMBERS TACKLED BY THE R.A.F. The pictures above, taken from fighters by a camera arranged to operate simultaneously with the firing of the plane's gun, show how the German raiders looked to British pilots sent up to intercept them. Top, part of an approaching formation of Heinkel "111's"; centre, left, Heinkels amid a rain of bullets; centre, right, a Dornier at close range; bottom, a Heinkel on the edge of an intense field of fire, indicated by tracer streaks.

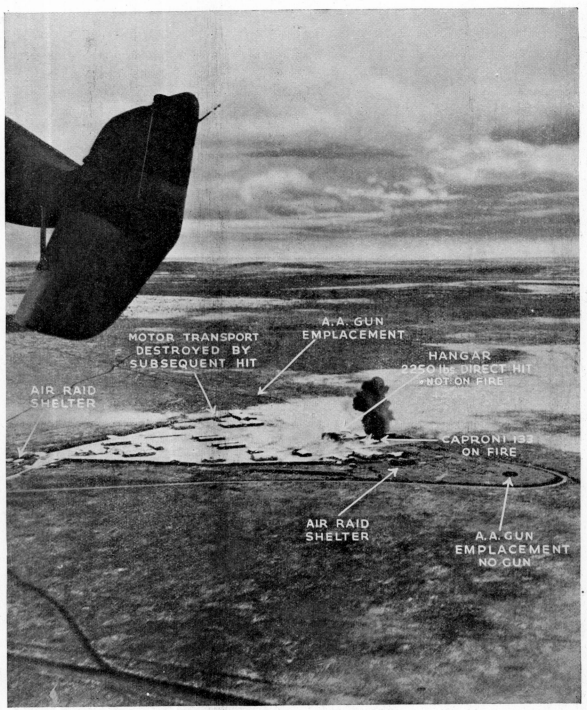

MOTOR TRANSPORT
DESTROYED BY
SUBSEQUENT HIT

A.A. GUN
EMPLACEMENT

HANGAR
2250 lbs DIRECT HIT
NOT ON FIRE

AIR RAID
SHELTER

CAPRONI 133
ON FIRE

AIR RAID
SHELTER

A.A. GUN
EMPLACEMENT
NO GUN

ATTACKING ITALY'S AFRICAN EMPIRE. Large-scale air attacks on Italy's possessions in Somaliland, Eritrea and Abyssinia by South African and British airmen were continuous during September. Much damage was done to the Jibuti-Addis Ababa railway, and countless hits were scored on aerodromes and other military objectives. In the picture a dense column of smoke is seen rising from a Caproni bomber set on fire by a bomb at one of these airfields. A hangar beside the column of smoke was destroyed by two direct hits.

General de Gaulle at Dakar

FREE FRENCH OFF WEST AFRICA. General de Gaulle, leader of the Free French, arrived off Dakar on 23 September with a small naval and military force. He hoped to enlist the support of the Colony against the Vichy government's policy of co-operation with Germany and persuade it to rally to the Free French standard. British ships stood by, but de Gaulle's attempt at a peaceful landing was resisted, and after two days he decided to withdraw rather than cause a fight between Frenchmen. British ships came into action, and two submarines which attacked them were sunk. The pictures show: above, General de Gaulle conferring with his officers before the withdrawal; below, French officers putting off to meet the French Governor-General in the town. The launch was fired on during its journey.

Italian bomber's watery grave

AIR BATTLES OFF LIBYAN COAST. During September Italy launched severa' air attacks on British naval units operating in the Mediterranean in an effort to justify her claims to the mastery of that sea. The Royal Air Force and the Navy combined to beat off the raiders, who showed no strong inclination to press the attacks home. The pictures show: above, an Italian bomber brought down by A.A. fire from a British warship during one of these attacks, its wings awash; below, left, the floating parachute of the ıtalian pilot, who came down in the sea; right, the pilot himself, kept afloa. by his life jacket, waits to be rescued by a British destroyer.

WATCHDOGS OF THE R.A.F. The planes and flying boats of the Coastal Command constantly patrolled vast areas of sea on the lookout for enemy U-boats and surface raiders lying in wait for British convoys. Altogether during 1940 they flew some twenty-five million miles and escorted over 2,000 convoys, including more than 40,000 ships carrying cargoes valued at an average of £4,000,000 per day. The "Sunderland" flying boat seen in the composite picture above has just bombed and sunk an Italian submarine whilst on patrol in the Mediterranean. All that can be seen of the under-water raider is a large patch of bubbles in the sea below.

R.A.F. HAVOC AT GERMAN NAVAL BASE. The harbour of Kiel, at the eastern end of the Kaiser Wilhelm Canal, Germany's most important naval port and dockyard, afforded an excellent target for the R.A.F., and one which they very frequently visited. Several large-scale attacks were made on it during September, resulting in considerable damage to shipping docked or under construction, and the results of the raids were evidenced by air photographs taken at various stages of the attacks. That reproduced above was taken two days after a particularly heavy raid in which much damage was done, and bombs were observed to fall close to the "Scharnhorst," Germany's crack 26,000-ton battleship, seen in floating dock at (1) in the picture. Other reference numbers indicate : (2) A 19,250-ton aircraft-carrier, not yet completed. (3) The heavy cruiser

OUTER DOCKYARD BASIN

NAVAL ARSENAL

"Lutzow," in dry dock, undergoing repairs to her stern. (4) A 10,000-ton cruiser of the "Hipper" class, also being repaired. (5) A smaller cruiser, in the repairers' hands. (6) Three submarines. (7) Two cruiser mine-layers. (8) Four torpedo-boats. (9) Three more submarines. (10) Two sail training ships. (11) A destroyer, in dry dock, undergoing repair. (12, 13, 15, 17) Tankers. (14, 16) Liners. (18) Destroyer, under construction. (19) Submarine, in floating dock. (20) Two submarines. (21) Light cruiser, under construction. (22) Submarine, in floating dock. (23) The target ship "Zahringen." (24) "E"-boats. Damage was also done to oil, torpedo and gun stores, and to the Central Power Station of the Deutsche Werke yard. Photographs taken a few days later showed that the "Scharnhorst" was undergoing repairs as a result of injuries sustained in the raids.

Japan signs pact with the Axis

TRIPARTITE TREATY SIGNED IN BERLIN. On 27 September, 1940, Japan, whose sympathies lay with Germany and Italy, signed a ten-year pact with these two countries. This provided for mutual aid in the event of any of the signatories being attacked by a power not so far involved in the war, and was interpreted as a warning to the United States. The picture above shows: left to right, seated, Ciano (Italy), Ribbentrop (Germany) and Saburo Kuruso (Japanese Ambassador to Germany) putting their signatures to the agreement. On the left Japanese officers on a mission to Germany are being shown the captured Maginot Line.

AIR ATTACKS ON VITAL RAILWAY CENTRE. A favourite target for the heavy bombers of the R.A.F. was the railway marshalling yard at Hamm, on the River Lippe. More than seventy raids had been made on this important objective by mid autumn, and considerable dislocation of Germany's rail traffic resulted. No sooner had the damaged lines and goods sheds been repaired than they were rendered useless once more by new attacks. This air photograph shows a stick of bombs falling on the yard during one of the September raids.

HOLBORN

ADEL

STRAND

OXFOR

PLACE

REGENT STREET

REET

THE NATIONAL BANK

TEMPLE

BOMB BLAST AT WESTMINSTER. Throughout the autumn, the nightly rain of high explosive bombs on London continued and many famous buildings suffered damage. Among them were the Houses of Parliament, one window of which, as seen above, has been damaged by the blast of a nearby bomb and has lost much of its tracery. Marochetti's statue of Richard Lionheart, outside, defies the enemy with sword bent but still unbroken.

Bomb damage in St. Paul's Cathedral

LONDON'S MOTHER CHURCH SUFFERS AGAIN. St. Paul's Cathedral, saved from destruction in the previous month by the heroic work of Lieut. Davies and his bomb disposal squad, continued to be a military objective for Nazi planes. In October it was seriously damaged by a high explosive bomb which pierced the roof and fell close to the High Altar which, as this picture shows, was reduced to a heap of rubble.

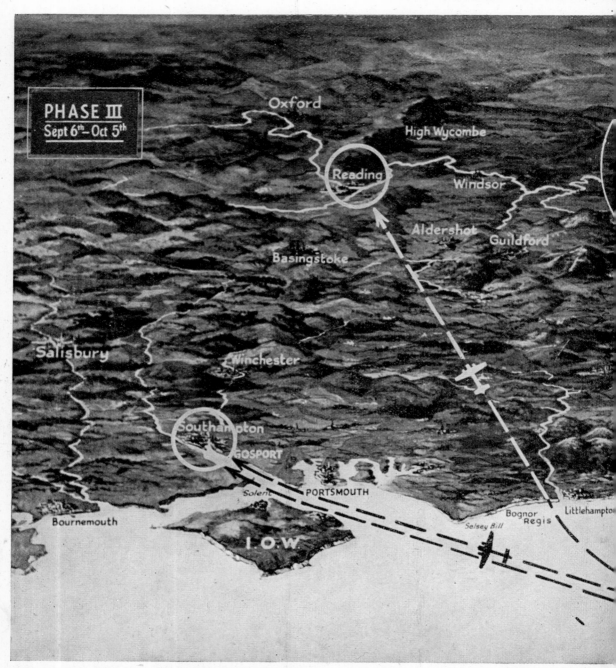

PHASE III
Sept 6th – Oct 5th

LONDON BECOMES LUFTWAFFE'S MAIN TARGET. The third stage of the Battle of Britain opened on 6 September, its first spectacular exploit being the mass attack on the London dockland area already described on pages 22 to 24. From the beginning of this phase to its end on 5 October, thirty-eight major daytime attacks were delivered, apart from the almost incessant night raids on the capital. Much damage was inflicted on private property, communications, and public utility services, but objectives of military importance suffered very little harm. The high-water mark of this phase of the contest came in the two great attacks on 15 September when the Germans lost 185 aircraft (see page 40). During the mass attacks dive bombers sought to create diversions by bombing shipping and coastal objectives in Essex and Kent. The fighter escorts of the attackers were increased in number, and endeavoured to draw off the defending R.A.F. fighter planes by flying high

Britain: The attacks on London

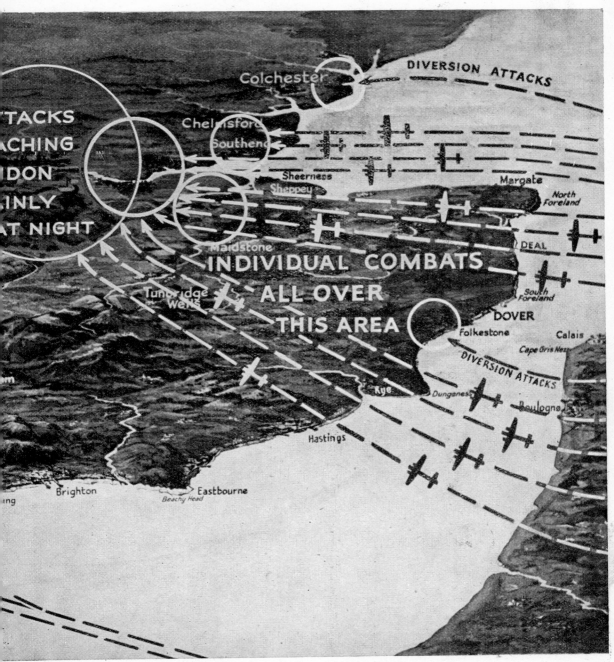

above their companion bombers. The R.A.F.'s reply to these tactics was for "Spitfire" squadrons to engage the high-flying fighter screen between London and the coast, while "Hurricanes" attacked the bombers before they reached the aerodromes in the London district. As the attacks continued, the proportion of German to British losses rose higher and higher; on 27 September one R.A.F. group destroyed 99 German aircraft for the loss of sixteen British pilots, while on 5 October only one pilot was shot down for an enemy loss of sixteen planes. The total loss of enemy machines in this third phase of the combat amounted to 883 aircraft. The map above, reproduced from the Air Ministry's official story of those historic days, "The Battle of Britain," shows the direction and objectives of the main and diversion attacks at this stage; the great bulk of the fighting took place over Kent and south-east Sussex, frequently centring on Tunbridge Wells and the surrounding area.

55

Free French standard raised at Duala

FRENCH COLONIES ADHERE TO DE GAULLE. Undaunted by lack of success at Dakar, the Free French leader continued to receive the adhesion of other French colonies in Africa and elsewhere to the cause of liberty. On 10 October his standard was raised at Duala, the capital of French Cameroon. The upper picture was taken as his expedition came alongside the quay at that town; below, troops pledged to the Free French cause parade for a war memorial ceremony at Noumea, in New Caledonia, the French island in the South Pacific.

Navy bombards Cherbourg

ENEMY SHIPS BATTERED IN NORMAN PORT. One of the most successful of the many remarkable operations aga nst the Channel ports was the Royal Navy's attack on a concentration of enemy shipping at Cherbourg, carried out in close co-operation with the R.A.F. An intense night bombardment by heavy and light naval units resulted in a large number of fires in the dock area. Havoc was wrought among the enemy vessels anchored in the harbour as the salvos from the British ships burst on their targets with unerring accuracy.

BRITISH NAVAL SUCCESS IN MEDITERRANEAN. On 12 October, H.M.S. "Ajax," which played a leading part in the battle of the River Plate, intercepted and sank two Italian destroyers off Sicily. A little later she met a force comprising a heavy cruiser and four destroyers, one of them, the 1,620-ton "Artigliere," of the latest class. "Ajax" after crippling this vessel was joined by H.M.S. "York," but lost her prey during the night.

Next morning "Artigliere" was located in tow of another Italian destroyer, which deserted her charge. "Artigliere's" crew was ordered to abandon ship, after which she was sunk by "York." The pictures show: top, left, the doomed ship after her crew have taken off; bottom, left, "York's" first salvo hits "Artigliere"; top, right, another shell striking the Italian vessel; bottom, right, the explosion after a direct hit on her magazine.

59

MORE MOVES ON DIPLOMATIC FRONT. On 23 October, in search of new Axis partners, Hitler met the Spanish dictator General Franco (top left) on the Spanish border, and the next day met Petain whom he is greeting (bottom) in France. The Vichy government afterwards announced that the German and French leaders had "agreed in principle" on collaboration. The meeting with the Spanish leader produced little result. Top, right, Hitler and Mussolini at the Palazzo Vecchio, Florence, where they conferred just before the Italian attack on Greece.

SENUSSI CHIEF ESCAPES FROM LIBYA. Among the native leaders opposed to the Italianization of Libya, Sayyid Idris el Senussi, head of the Senussi sect of Mohammedans, had long been prominent. In October, as leader of a Free Libyan movement, he made his way from Italian territory into Egypt, where he is seen (above) with an escort of his followers and accompanied by British and Egyptian officers as he passes a guard of honour of Indian troops. Below, a group of Libyan prisoners of war kneel at prayer during his visit to their camp.

C.P.R. FLAGSHIP DESTROYED BY AIR ATTACK. The "Empress of Britain," crack 42,000-ton liner of the Canadian Pacific Fleet, was attacked by enemy aircraft on 26 October about 150 miles from the Irish coast. After machine gunning the liner's gun crew the German dive bombers registered direct hits with both high explosive and incendiary bombs, leaving the vessel a blazing wreck (right). The tugs seen to the left

attempted to tow her to port, but the effort was unsuccessful, and the liner, with flames belching from her funnels, blew up and sank in the darkness. Some 600 of the 643 souls aboard, who included military families and a small number of military personnel, were picked up and brought to port by British naval vessels. Among the rescued was the commander, Captain Sapsworth, C.V.O., who remained with his ship till she sank.

GREEKS REJECT ITALIAN ULTIMATUM. Italy, alleging violations of Greek neutrality, presented a three-hour ultimatum to Greece on 28 October, demanding that certain unspecified strategical points be conceded. The Greek Premier, Gen. Metaxas, received this as a declaration of war. An Italian attack was immediately launched. The pictures show: top, left, Greek first-line troops watching the Albanian frontier a few days before war was declared; right, Greek troops in action near the frontier; bottom, left, Italian cavalry riding into Greece; right, Greek warships which shelled the Italian forces near the coast as they sought to cross the Albanian border into Greek territory.

THE BATTLE OF LONDON.
Throughout October the Nazi attack on London continued in a fruitless endeavour to break the spirit of its people, and to raze their homes and historic buildings to the ground. The "military objectives" attacked by the Germans included hospitals, churches, museums, the halls of City companies, cinemas and restaurants, mansions, blocks of flats, and the working-class dwellings of the little streets. Typical scenes of those memorable days are depicted in these photographs. They show (1) "The Times" office, in Queen Victoria Street, its windows and much of its walls damaged by blast, but with its flags still bravely flying. (2) The Dutch Church, Austin

Friars, dating from before London's first Great Fire in 1666, completely ruined and burnt out. (3) The library of Holland House, Lord Ilchester's Kensington mansion, once the home of Charles James Fox, which with the exception of one wing was completely destroyed. (4) St. Clement Danes, the famous church in the Strand, badly damaged by blast from a heavy bomb. (5) Damage in Middle Temple Hall, opened by Queen Elizabeth in 1562. (6) Leicester Square, where Thurston's, the famous billiard centre, was ruined. (7) The main hall of Stationers' Hall, showing the Caxton window, part of which was destroyed. (8) Pensioners surveying bomb damage at the Royal Hospital, Chelsea.

LONDON LAUGHS AT THE BLITZ. Loss of sleep, nights in underground shelters, homelessness—nothing could take the smile from the Londoners' faces. After the raid they came out from their refuge to salve whatever could be rescued of their treasured possessions—even if it were only a clock or an aspidistra.

Raid damage in S.E. London

LONDON SCENES AFTER A RAID. Not only hundreds of lives but the furniture and treasures of many humble homes were saved by the untiring efforts of the rescue workers. Above, a pile of salvaged furniture is waiting in a working-class street to be claimed by its owners. Below, ruined dwelling-houses and shops in the famous South London thoroughfare, Old Kent Road, a short time after one of the heavy October raids.

SOUTH AFRICAN PREMIER VISITS UNION TROOPS. In October and November General Smuts made a tour of inspection of Union troops at their advanced training camps in East Africa, where they were preparing for forthcoming operations against the Italians in Abyssinia, Eritrea and Italian and British Somaliland. The pictures show: above, troops giving their Premier a rousing reception after hearing a speech from him during his visit; below, part of a troop-carrying convoy of highly-mechanized South African units in Kenya.

ITALIAN ADVANCE IN GREECE HELD. Italian troops that invaded Greek territory had been promised an easy victory by the Duce, but within the first few days they were to learn that they were opposed by a brave and resolute enemy who could take full advantage of the difficult and rugged country. The pictures, taken during the early days of the campaign, show: above, Italians retreating along a mountain road after a Greek counter-attack; below, Greek infantry on the march to take up their positions in the line.

BRITISH SUPPORT FOR INVADED GREECE. Before the war began, Britain and France had promised to aid Greece if attacked. Britain's promise was at once kept and air and land forces were dis- embarked in Greece and Crete to support her in her struggle for freedom. The pictures show: top, left, British troops and tanks being blessed by a Cretan bishop as they pass through a town in the island; bottom, crowds in a Greek town watching a newly-arrived British mechanized column; top right, General Sir A. Wavell (in centre) visiting a gun position in course of erection by British troops; bottom, R.A.F. personnel, with their kit, newly landed in Greece from a British warship.

BRITAIN'S REPLY TO ITALY. Activity in the Eastern theatres of war increased as autumn advanced, and the growing naval and air forces of the Commonwealth scored many brilliant successes. Heavy and successful bombing attacks from the air were repeatedly made on enemy positions and troop concentrations in Libya and Italian East Africa; and several Italian naval vessels and supply ships were sunk in the Red Sea and Mediterranean, including a destroyer and two submarines. The pictures on the left tell the story of an Italian

submarine's fate.   Top, she is forced to surface by a destroyer's depth charges, only to meet an attack from a British flying boat.   Centre, she is settling by the stern under the combined assault of the destroyer's shells and the plane's bombs.   Below, a last sight of the vessel as she disappears beneath the waves.   Right, top, a patrol of "Hurricanes" in the Middle East breaks for action as enemy aircraft are reported near; bottom, native boys inspect with interest the wreckage of an Italian plane shot down by South African airmen in Kenya.

"JERVIS BAY'S" HEROIC ACTION.   On 12 November the Admiralty told the true story of a sea encounter that had taken place a week earlier in the North Atlantic, in which Germany claimed to have sunk an entire British convoy.   A surface raider, thought to be a pocket battleship, had attacked a convoy of thirty-eight ships. Thirty-two of these, however, arrived safely in port, mainly owing to the gallant action of the armed merchant

cruiser "Jervis Bay," whose Commander, Capt. Fogarty Fegen, gave battle in spite of the attacker's far heavier armament. Heavily hit and set on fire early in the action, the "Jervis Bay" closed with the enemy, holding German fire long enough to enable her charges to escape. After about three hours of battle she sank. Her captain was posthumously awarded the V.C. This drawing, by Rowland Hilder, R.I., vividly portrays the action.

AMERICA CHOOSES BETWEEN TWO FRIENDS OF BRITAIN. On election day in November the American people went to the polls to choose their President for the next four years.   The choice lay between Franklin Roosevelt, staunch friend of Britain's cause, who had already occupied the White House for eight years, and Wendell Willkie, equally pledged by his programme to give all aid short of war to the forces of Democracy: the only point at issue was the form that aid should take.   Roosevelt received 27,200,000 votes

to Willkie's 22,300,000, gaining a majority in thirty-nine of the forty-eight states of the Union, and thus becoming the first president to be elected for a third successive term; and his opponent, in a speech immediately after the election, declared that his supporters would stand behind the newly-elected President in carrying out the policy which the nation had endorsed. Left, thousands of Willkie supporters with banners take part in a campaign march; right, Mr. Roosevelt addressing a New York crowd at his last pre-election meeting.

HITLER THREATENS BUT DOESN'T COME.

Continual threats of an imminent invasion of Britain appeared in the German Press and the speeches of German leaders, and German land forces trained intensively for the difficult job of getting and keeping a foothold on British shores. Left, Nazi soldiers are scaling cliffs over terrain such as they would meet on the English and Scottish coasts; a light gun team are seen hauling up their weapon. Right, above, Goering, with (left) Gen. Jeschonnek, Chief of the German Air Staff, and (right) Air Force Gen. Loerzer, making plans, with the aid of a map, for an attack on Britain. Below, a heavy bomb, which will fall on some British target, on its way to be loaded at an airfield in France.

BRITAIN PREPARES A HOT RECEPTION.

Meanwhile, a warm welcome was in preparation for the invaders—if they came. Not only was a great army ready to meet them, but the rapidly-growing Home Guards were intensively training in every town and village, eager for a chance to show what they could do to keep Britain free. The pictures show: top, left, motor cyclist troops in training; bottom, left, Home Guard armoured car exercises; top, right, a tank assembly park at a home training school of the Royal Armoured Corps; centre, one of the heavy guns that would batter the invading forces if they ever gave it the opportunity; bottom, an A.A. gun in action at an air defence training school.

ITALIAN ADVANCE HALTED. The Italian thrust into Greece towards Salonika was held three miles over the frontier, and within a few days Greek troops, counterattacking, hurled the enemy back into Albania. By November 5 Koritza was within range of Greek mountain artillery. Meanwhile two Italian attacks further west, designed to encircle Yanina, were brought to a standstill by the Greeks. The pictures show: top, left, Italian troops in full retreat, their mechanical transport abandoned, urging on a mule wagon. Bottom, left, engineers building a temporary bridge to replace one destroyed by the R.A.F. Top, right, light tanks captured by the Greeks, who used them against their former owners. Bottom, right, Italian guns and mortars captured during the Greek advance.

ITALIAN REVERSE IN EAST AFRICA. Fort Gallabat, a post on the Abyssinia-Sudan frontier, was taken by the Italians in July. Early in November, however, British and Indian troops launched an attack on the post, which changed hands several times before finally falling to the British on 7 November, the Italian forces retreating towards Metemma harassed by aerial bombardment. The pictures show: top, British troops in possession of the fort on the lookout for enemy movements; below, artillery shelling the fort before its final capture.

ITALIAN PLANES OVER BRITAIN. On Armistice Day Britain received the first large-scale visit from the Italian Air Force. Between fifteen and twenty bombers that appeared over the Thames Estuary, escorted by about sixty fighters, were routed by two "Hurricane" squadrons, who shot down eight bombers and five fighters without loss to themselves. Two of the planes, a Caproni bomber (above) and a Fiat "C.R. 42" fighter (below), both of which crashed in Suffolk, are here shown. The remainder of the Italian formation dropped their bombs in the sea and fled.

CRIPPLING BLOW AT DUCE'S NAVY. On the night of 11-12 November a magnificently conceived attack on Italian capital ships in Taranto harbour was made by torpedo-carrying planes from the aircraft-carriers "Eagle" and "Illustrious." Its results decisively altered the balance of naval power in the Mediterranean. The victorious planes returned to their base leaving two battleships, one of the 35,000-ton "Littorio" class and

one of the 23,000-ton "Cavour" class, partly under water, and another "Cavour" class battleship severely damaged. Two cruisers were seen with a bad list to starboard; and two fleet auxiliaries had their sterns under water. Only two British machines were lost in the action. The picture, specially drawn by Frank Mason, R.I., R.O.I., shows the British planes swooping to launch their torpedoes with the greatest possible accuracy.

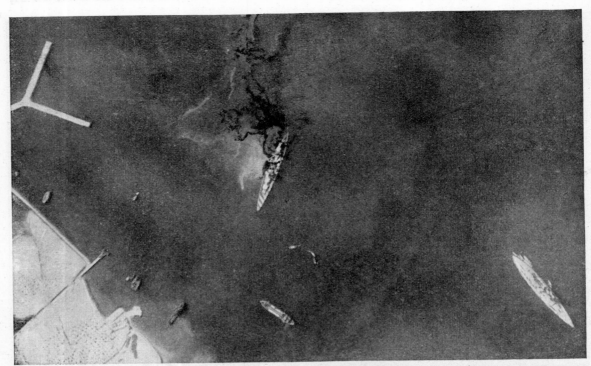

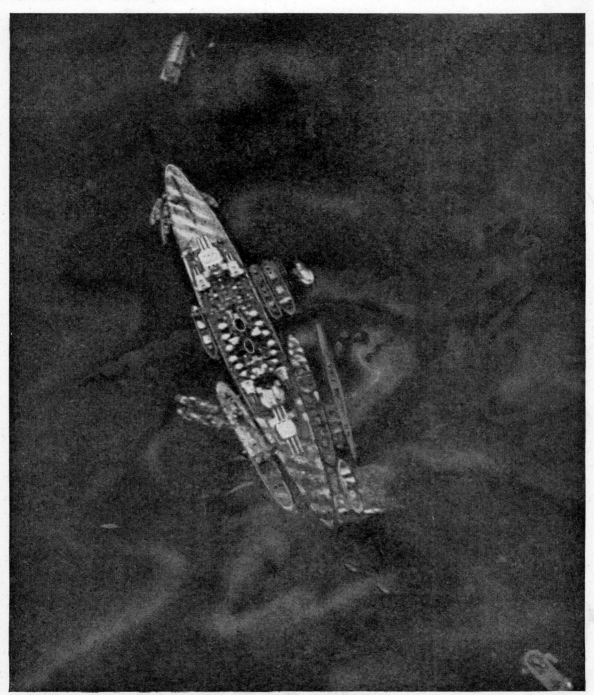

FLEET AIR ARM'S EXPLOIT AT TARANTO. The success of the Taranto attack was verified in subsequent reconnaissance flights by British planes, which showed that two of the damaged battleships were aground and the third apparently abandoned. Photographs taken during these flights show: on the left, above, a "Cavour" class battleship, her starboard side and her stern aft of the rear gun turrets submerged, beached on the outer harbour. Below, the inner harbour, with two damaged cruisers of the "Trento" class, and other warships; large quantities of oil fuel can be seen floating on the surface of the water. Above, a "Littorio" class battleship badly down by the bows, with salvage vessels and tugs and naval repair ships alongside.

TORPEDO–CARRIERS AND THEIR FLOATING HOME. Italy's fast but very shy navy always showed itself anxious to avoid meeting the British fleet in open battle. Admiral Sir Andrew Cunningham, Commander of the British Mediterranean Fleet, was therefore forced to destroy it while it lay at anchor at its base. In the "glorious episode of Taranto," to use Mr. Winston Churchill's words, he employed aircraft carriers, from the decks of which torpedo-carrying planes could take off to seek out the enemy. The success of the attack

proved beyond doubt the value of these ships, and brought fresh honour to the Fleet Air Arm, whose offensive action against the Italian fleet in the Mediterranean had already won them high praise. Torpedo-carriers can carry either a load of bombs or a single 18-in. torpedo. Left, one of these machines is seen releasing its "tin fish" during a practice flight. Right, above, a "Swordfish," wings folded, passing down the aft lift well of its parent ship. Below, one of the planes circling round the aircraft-carrier "Ark Royal" preparatory to landing.

WANTON DESTRUCTION OF COVENTRY. A ruthless attack was made by the Luftwaffe on Coventry on the night of 14 November. Relays of bombers flew over the city from nightfall to dawn, dropping hundreds of tons of bombs indiscriminately and reducing the beautiful fourteenth-century Cathedral to a shapeless pile of stones. Churches, hospitals, cinemas, public buildings, and many shops and houses in the business centre and outskirts were destroyed or badly damaged. Left, the Cathedral spire, happily still standing, looks sadly down on the wreckage below; part of the walls and interior of the ruined Cathedral are shown in the picture on right (above), while below is seen the damaged font.

COVENTRY AFTER THE RAID.   The German wireless, gloating over the havoc wrought in Coventry by their bombers, coined a new word, "coventrated," to describe what Goering's raiders had done to the city.

But the spirit of Coventry's people may be judged from the Mayor's remark on seeing the damage caused in the business centre (above): "We've always wanted a site for a new civic centre," he said, "and now we have it.".

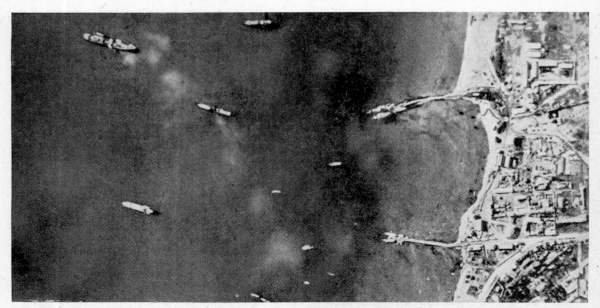

BRITISH AIR AID FOR GREECE. While the Greek troops thrust the Italians back into the Albanian mountains, British bombers rained their missiles on the retreating armies—and their bases. These pictures show the harbour of Valona before and during an R.A.F. raid. Here men and supplies from Bari, on the Italian coast opposite, were disembarked. The explosions on the jetty in the lower picture show the accuracy of the bombing.

R.A.F. bomb objectives in Eritrea

BOMBS ON ITALY'S OLDEST COLONY. Eritrea, the coastal strip on the Red Sea which had been in Italy's hands since 1890, was one of several East African theatres in which the R.A.F. were very active. The pictures above show an area at Mai Edaga, Gura, before and after a bombing attack. Comparison of the buildings and roads numbered one to six in the two pictures shows the extent of the damage effected by a single raid.

ALBANIA'S LARGEST TOWN IN GREEK HANDS. The Greek counter-attack in Eastern Albania pushed the Italians gradually but relentlessly back towards Koritza, and the capture of that town was announced by the Greek High Command on the 22nd. Many prisoners and numerous guns were taken. The pictures show: above, a Greek mule transport column moving along an Albanian mountain road; below, Greek troops preparing to bivouac for the night among the snows, whose rigours they could withstand far better than their foes.

Navy convoys equipment to Greece

BRITISH HELP ON ITS WAY. Britain's promised aid to Greece was not limited to support in the air. Many a convoy, such as that seen above, passed through Mussolini's "private" Mediterranean with stores and equipment for the Greek and British Forces operating on the Albanian frontier. They were not immune from Italian air attack, but enemy bombers seldom succeeded in inflicting on them anything more than "near misses." Below, "Ark Royal," "Malaya" and "Renown," engaged on convoy duty, passing the Rock of Gibraltar.

NAVAL ACTION IN MEDITERRANEAN. On 27 November British naval and Fleet Air Arm forces made contact with two enemy battleships escorted by cruisers and destroyers to the west of Sardinia. Though the Italian ships opened fire, they soon broke off the action and retired, a cruiser, two destroyers and other vessels being seriously damaged before their escape. One British fighter plane was lost, and H.M. cruiser "Berwick" suffered slight damage. Above, a British destroyer firing at the Italian ships as enemy shells fall astern. Below, a British destroyer and cruisers are taking up their positions before the beginning of the action.

King visits bombed Southampton

AIR TERROR IN THE PROVINCES. After the conclusion of the Battle of Britain at the end of October, the German Air Force changed their tactics and launched heavy night attacks on ports and industrial towns in the provinces. One of the most severe was a raid on Southampton on 30 November. The business centre of the city bore the brunt of the attack. Churches, shops, houses, a cinema and a newspaper office were among the buildings hit. A few days later the King visited the stricken city. He is seen above, accompanied by Mr. Herbert Morrison, and the mayor of the city, inspecting the damage while troops are still clearing up.

Scenes in London during

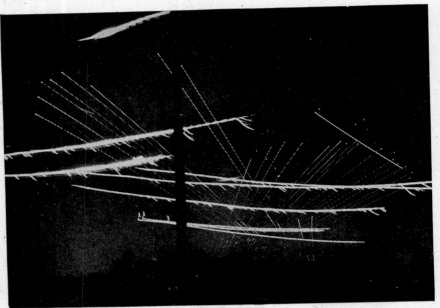

NIGHT RAIDS ON LONDON CONTINUE. Heavy air attacks were made on London on the 12, 15 and 29 November. Many fires were started, and fire fighters had a busy time keeping the outbreaks under control. These pictures show: left, parachute flares dropped by the raiders to illuminate the target area mingling with gun flashes and tracer shells. Below, firemen tackling a blaze in a city building and (top right) playing their hoses on a fire in a city street. Bottom right, the Old Bailey, St. Martin's, Ludgate, and St. Paul's Cathedral brilliantly illuminated by a nearby fire.

THE CHANGING FACE OF LONDON. By the end of November many of London's most famous landmarks, churches, hospitals, theatres, cinemas, stores, and other public buildings showed signs of the nightly air bombardment. A few of those damaged in November raids are shown here. Top left, part of the Tower of London after a raid— the eight-hundred-year-old walls appear to defy Hitler no less successfully than the steel and concrete of the twentieth century. Bottom, the famous and fashionable church of St. James, Piccadilly. Top right, the Houses of Parliament, where damage was done to the cloisters and crypt; bottom, the auditorium of Drury Lane Theatre, where a bomb exploded at the back of the pit.

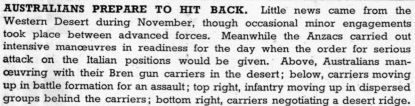

AUSTRALIANS PREPARE TO HIT BACK. Little news came from the Western Desert during November, though occasional minor engagements took place between advanced forces. Meanwhile the Anzacs carried out intensive manœuvres in readiness for the day when the order for serious attack on the Italian positions would be given. Above, Australians man-œuvring with their Bren gun carriers in the desert; below, carriers moving up in battle formation for an assault; top right, infantry moving up in dispersed groups behind the carriers; bottom right, carriers negotiating a desert ridge.

30 NOVEMBER—4 DECEMBER, 1940: ITALIANS BACK IN GREECE—AS PRISONERS. After the capture of Koritza, the Greeks pushed on in Eastern Albania towards Pogradets, the capture of which was announced on 30 November. Four days later came the news that the town of Premeti had fallen to the Greek Army advancing from the Pindus. Every day hundreds of prisoners fell, many of them willingly enough, into Greek hands. Here, in a Greek concentration camp, is a batch of them, lining up for rations.

AIR ATTACKS ON GREEK CIVILIANS. The Italians, in the face of the unexpectedly successful resistance of the hardy mountain troops, resorted to terror tactics in the air. The tiny Greek Air Force, magnificently as it fought, could do little to mitigate the effects of ruthless attacks on civilians. Above, an Italian photograph of a bombing raid on Yanina, the town which the Italians had unsuccessfully attempted to encircle at the beginning of their invasion. Below, shattered houses in the little town of Kastoria, to the south-east of Koritza.

TWO IMPORTANT GREEK VICTORIES. Santi Quaranta, the Italians' southernmost Albanian sea base, was occupied on 5 December by the Greek Army advancing along the coastal road. On the same day the Italians evacuated Argyrokastro, which was entered by the Greeks, advancing through Delvino, on 8 December. Many prisoners and much war material were taken by the victors in both cases. Above, Greek airmen about to take off for a bombing raid on Italian positions; below, a view of the town and harbour of Santi Quaranta.

7 DECEMBER, 1940: H.M.S. "KELLY" IN SERVICE AGAIN. The British flotilla leader "Kelly" was torpedoed off the German coast in May. Badly damaged, she was towed across the North Sea to England, where she underwent repair. The first intimation of her adventure was the announcement made in December that she was again on active service. This picture, taken from another warship, shows members of her crew being transferred to another vessel.

GERMAN BLOCKADE-RUNNER SUNK OFF CUBA. On 8 December the 5,000-ton "Idarwald" was intercepted off Cuba by H.M.S. "Diomede." Her crew at once scuttled her, set her on fire and took to the boats. A party from the British ship boarded her, fought the fire (right, below) and got it under control, but the freighter was past salvation; she soon had to be cast off, and sank. Above, a boarding party from "Diomede" approach the burning ship. Right (top), "Diomede" comes alongside "Idarwald" as she settles in the water.

MENACE TO EGYPT CHECKED. The lull in the Western Desert which had followed on the Italian capture of Sollum and Sidi Barrani in September was rudely broken on 9 December. At dawn on that day General Wavell's army began a general offensive. Two hours later the Italian camp at Nibeiwa, fifteen miles from Sidi Barrani, had been captured, 500 prisoners taken, and General Maletti, commander of these Italian advanced troops, killed. The attack had been preceded by a heavy bombing raid the previous night on all the Italian

airfields along the Libyan coast, seriously reducing Italy's air power in North Africa; and during the first day of the advance twenty-two Italian planes—and one British—were lost. Left, an Italian field gun put out of action and captured during the advance; the surrounding litter and dead gunner show how quickly it was abandoned. Above, a R.A.F. bomb exploding near an Italian convoy in the desert. Though most of the troops attacked have fallen flat, one machine gunner, less cautious than his comrades, is still firing at the British plane.

INVADERS EXPELLED FROM EGYPT.   General Wavell's offensive pushed forward with amazing success. On 11 December Sidi Barrani was reoccupied, and three Italian generals, with many other prisoners, were taken.   On 16 December Sollum fell again into British hands, and Egypt was freed from the invader.   Anzacs and Indian troops played a great part in the victorious advance.   The pictures show: above, Italian prisoners, mostly destined for internment in India, being marched away under guard of a few British soldiers; below, some of the piles of stores and equipment left behind by the enemy in their flight being loaded on to captured Italian lorries by Italian prisoners.   Right, above, a 25-pounder gun-howitzer, protected by a dust cover from the sand, passing through Sidi Barrani; below, a signpost at Sollum pointing the way for the next British advance.

16 DECEMBER, 1940: BRITISH ENTER LIBYA. After taking over 30,000 prisoners in Egypt Wavell's victorious army crossed the border into Libya, and occupied Fort Capuzzo, south of Bardia, a frequent mark in the past for British air attacks and the first Libyan post to fall into British hands. Advance armoured forces are here seen passing the Fort.

British recapture Fort Wajir

16 December, 1940

NEW PUSH IN EAST AFRICA. The frontier post of El Wak, near the border of Italian Somaliland, had been occupied by the Italians during their advance into Kenya in the summer, together with the fort and well of Wajir, to the south-west. On 16 December Wajir was retaken, and El Wak raided, by a South African force, who rendered it unusable by the enemy, capturing a number of prisoners, with guns, ammunition, and food stores. West African troops from the Gold Coast, who played a large part by the side of the Union soldiers in these operations, are seen above training their rifles on the enemy, and (below) marching past Wajir.

GERMAN INDUSTRIAL CENTRE BOMBED. Mannheim, great industrial centre of south-west Germany, was subjected to a particularly intense series of attacks by the R.A.F. on the nights of 16, 17 and 18 December. Thousands of incendiary and high explosive bombs were dropped and many fires started. The picture, taken during one of the raids, shows: (1) Fires burning in the neighbourhood of the Central Station (shown at 3). (2) A large area in the centre of the industrial quarter well ablaze. (4) The railway marshalling yards.

BRITISH AIRMEN OVER GERMANY. While Nazi planes continued to raid British cities and towns, the R.A.F. struck with ever-increasing power at enemy military and industrial objectives. These pictures of night air operations show: top left, an air crew entering their plane to take off at the control officer's signal; bottom,

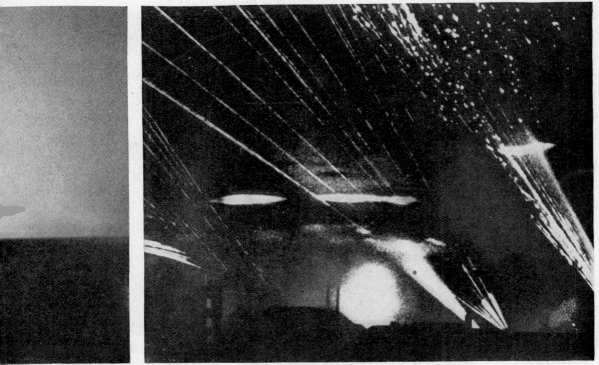

left, bombers silhouetted in the light of a flare used for recalling planes to their airfield; top right, bombers crossing the Dutch coast in the glare of searchlights; bottom right, night sky over Berlin, the blaze of a great fire showing the havoc wrought by the British machines despite the terrific display of shells and tracer bullets.

ARMY OF THE NILE IN LIBYA. The British offensive, begun in the Western Desert on 9 December with Naval and Air Force co-operation, produced magnificent results in an incredibly short time; and the Italian retreat soon became a rout. The coastal road at Sollum, nicknamed "Hell-Fire Pass," the Italians' only line of retreat, was heavily shelled, and on 15 December Imperial Forces crossed the frontier into Libya. Sollum was occupied on the 16th, and the Italians driven out of Egypt, leaving the way open for an attack on the fortified

seaport of Bardia, which Mussolini had called "a bastion of Fascism." By 18 December over 30,000 prisoners had been taken in the Libyan operations, in which Indian troops played a prominent part, especially at Sidi Barrani. As the land forces approached Bardia, the port was subjected to continual intense raiding by the R.A.F. Troops from Australia and New Zealand were in the forefront of the advance. Some of these are here seen taking shelter in a captured anti-tank ditch built by the Italians, while shells burst in Bardia.

SURROUNDING DOOMED BARDIA. The advance on Bardia by land and air forces began on 16 December. An inner circle of mobile units, supported by infantry and guns, closed up around the port, which was continually harassed by heavy artillery fire. The pictures show: top left, a howitzer, and right, artillery bombarding the town; bottom, giant tanks operating over the sandy wastes as the British forces close in

THE GREAT FIRE
OF LONDON

29 DECEMBER, 1940

Christmas brought an undeclared truce in the aerial
warfare over Britain, though there was some activity on
the nights of 27 and 28 December. On the night of the
29th came the explanation of the lull. Shortly after dark,
waves of raiders, flying over the heart of the City of London,
rained thousands of incendiary and explosive bombs on
its historic buildings in a deliberate effort to surpass the
effects of the Great Fire of 1666. St. Paul's, close-ringed
by flame, remained, as by a miracle, practically unharmed;
but many of Wren's famous churches, the five-hundred-
year-old Guildhall, banks, offices and shops by the hundred,
were reduced to ashes. All through the night, watchers
on the outskirts saw the great dome of London's cathedral
standing out against an awesome background of flame.
Yet, throughout that terrible night, the City's work went
on; as the fire services, police, and civil defence workers
toiled nobly at the risk of limb and life to fight the flames,
and civilians helped to tackle incendiary bombs before
they could start fresh fires, newspaper workers stayed at
their posts, amid the conflagration, so that there should
be no delay in the distribution of their papers in the morning.
Not till the next day, and hardly then, could the full extent
of the destruction be realized. In spite of the ferocity
of the assault, and although three hospitals were hit, human
casualties were surprisingly few. It was made known a
few days later that the attack would have been prolonged
and developed still more fiercely had not the sudden
development of bad weather over Northern France foiled
the plans of the Luftwaffe. Realizing that much of the damage
by incendiary bombs might have been avoided if they had
been dealt with immediately they fell, the Government
decided to make "fire-watching" compulsory and took
powers to conscript all employers and employees to share,
if necessary, in the protection of their places of work from fire
bombs. The picture shows buildings on the river bank, with
St. Paul's (right) and the slender spire of destroyed St. Bride's
silhouetted against the flames at the height of the raid.

THE CITY AFTER THE RAID. It was a battered London to which workers came on the morning after the raid. Miles of hose lay tangled everywhere; firemen and auxiliaries were still pouring powerful jets on unextinguished fires, and many workers had to tramp long distances before discovering whether their offices still stood. The pictures show: top, left, St. Paul's, seen through the ruined archway of a smouldering building; centre, fire-fighting appliances burnt out while tackling the flames; right, firemen at work in a main City street; bottom, left, office workers negotiating hoses on their way to work; right, firemen and soldiers, clambering over heaps of debris as they bring up more hose.

GUILDHALL WRECKED IN FIRE RAID. The City's civic centre, the ancient and historic Guildhall, begun in 1411 and remodelled by Wren after the first Great Fire, was in large part reduced to ruins as a result of the fires which broke out when sparks and burning timbers fell on its roof from the tower of the adjoining church of St. Lawrence Jewry. The famous banqueting hall, scene of the Lord Mayor's annual banquet on 9 November, is shown on the left; right, above, the entrance to the Council Chamber; below, the Lord Mayor surveying the damaged interior a few days after the raid.

W.I.P.2—E*

29 DECEMBER 1940: THE DESOLATED CITY. This picture, taken from the summit of St. Paul's, shows one of the areas where the Great Fire raged most fiercely. The shattered walls to the left were Paternoster Square; Newgate Street, Paternoster Row and Warwick Lane marked the limits of the area shown. There had been housed business firms whose names were known at the other end of the world

FIRE AND FLOOD AMONG THE BOOKS. Among the severest sufferers in London's fire raid were her book publishing businesses. Housed in old-fashioned buildings in the narrow streets near St. Paul's Cathedral their stocks of printed matter were easy prey for the flames, and it was estimated that during the night some three million volumes perished. In the ruins of Ave Maria Lane, shown above, lengths of hose lie among the charred fragments of the books which were for Goering's bombers a "military objective."

This was Paternoster Row

THE TRAIL OF THE DESTROYER. Paternoster Row, a little street running from Cheapside to Ave Maria Lane, almost too narrow for wheeled traffic, was London's Bible warehouse. Windows full of religious books alternated with tiny cafés where local office workers snatched a hurried meal at midday. On 28 December it was, as it had been for long years past, an oasis of comparative quiet and peace wedged between two main arteries of London's traffic. On the morning of Monday, 30 December, 1940, it looked like this.

29 DECEMBER 1940: A BLITZED CITY BACK-WATER. Here is Paternoster Square as the Germans left it. On the summit of the Old Bailey, in the background, the figure of Justice, blindfold, holds her balance and uplifted sword in the sight of the stricken City

MAKING WAR ON RELIGION AND BEAUTY. The queerly-named City churches, most of which had risen under the hand of Sir Christopher Wren from the ashes of the first Great Fire in 1666, suffered heavily in the second conflagration of 1940. Above, left, the interior of St. Bride's, Fleet Street, the church of newspaperland, famous for its slender spire, one of Wren's masterpieces; centre, the ruins of St. Mary the Virgin, Aldermanbury, where Shakespeare once habitually worshipped; right, All Hallows, Barking, famous in all English-speaking lands as the headquarters of Toc H: in the background is the "Crusaders' Chapel," with its destroyed altar. Below, left, all that was left of St. Giles', Cripplegate, the burial place of Milton, John Foxe, and the Elizabethan sailor, Martin Frobisher; this church, like All Hallows, Barking, survived the first Great Fire only to perish in the second. Centre, the ruins of Christchurch, Greyfriars, Newgate Street, where the "Bluecoat Boys" of Christ's Hospital held their annual commemorative service. Right, charred debris within the battered walls of the church of St. Andrew by the Wardrobe. Other churches seriously damaged include St. Lawrence Jewry, the "official" church of the City Corporation; St. Stephen, Coleman Street; St. Leonard Foster, and St. Mary Woolnoth.

30 DECEMBER 1940: SOLDIERS TAKE OVER CITY CLEARANCE. Troops were drafted into the City after the raid to clear the streets and demolish dangerous buildings. The picture shows the smoke of an explosion as a partly-burnt out building in Newgate Street is dynamited by Royal Engineers

COMPLETING CITY DEMOLITION. The urgent work of dealing with dangerous buildings in the City was largely undertaken by the Pioneer Corps. Left, members of the Corps are demolishing a wall during a tour of the blitzed area by their Commandant, Lord Milne. Right, Pioneers clear the debris from a main

thoroughfare beneath the pall of smoke and dust which still hangs over the gutted buildings.   The task of clearance was carried through with surprising speed, and within a few days communications had been restored, public services were working almost as usual, and business houses had re-established themselves in new offices.

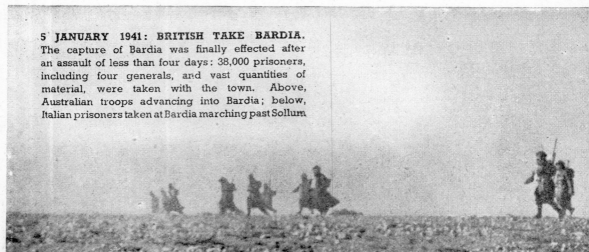

5 JANUARY 1941: BRITISH TAKE BARDIA.
The capture of Bardia was finally effected after an assault of less than four days: 38,000 prisoners, including four generals, and vast quantities of material, were taken with the town. Above, Australian troops advancing into Bardia; below, Italian prisoners taken at Bardia marching past Sollum

SOUTH COAST NAVAL BASES RAIDED. Intense night air attacks were made on Portsmouth on 10 January and on Plymouth three days later. Churches, hospitals and private dwellings were damaged in each case, and many persons rendered homeless. Left, top, the remains of St. Andrew's, Plymouth's mother church. Bottom, weary firemen at Plymouth, after fighting the flames all night, hoist the Union Jack on a lamp-post. Above, the funeral of some of the Portsmouth victims: twenty-five bodies are being buried in a common grave.

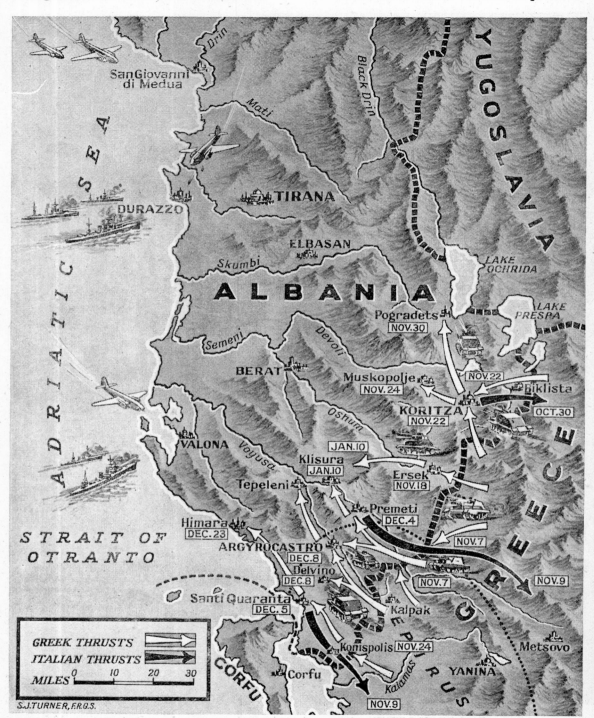

ALBANIAN CAMPAIGN. The map above shows the direction of the early Italian thrust into northern Greece, which reached its "farthest south" on 9 November, after crossing the Kalamas and, farther east, striking at Metsovo through the Sarandoporo valley. Here the crack Italian "Venezia Alpini" were cut off and isolated by the Greeks, who then became the attackers, first in the north-east towards Koritza and Pogradets, then in the centre towards Premeti and Klisura and finally along the coast in the direction of Santi Quaranta and Himara.

Mr. Willkie visits Britain

U.S. PRESIDENTIAL CANDIDATE IN ENGLAND. Mr. Wendell Willkie, Republican candidate in the Presidential election of 1940, arrived in England in January. He conferred with Mr. Churchill and other national leaders, visited defences and inspected bomb damage in London and the provinces, and reiterated his determination to do everything possible to aid Britain in his own country. Above, he is seen (right foreground) visiting a shelter during an air raid; below, enthusiastic crowds greet him as he leaves his car during a visit to Manchester.

RE-ELECTED AMERICAN PRESIDENT TAKES OFFICE. On 20 January, Franklin D. Roosevelt took the oath of office as President for the third time, and thus became the first man in the history of the United States to hold that office for three successive terms. His election was warmly welcomed in Britain, for the President,

an ardent Democrat, was opposed to the Nazi regime and was a warm supporter of Britain and her Allies in their fight for freedom.   Hundreds of tanks, rolling through Washington in the parade from the Capitol which concluded the inaugural ceremony, show that America is prepared to play her part in the defence of democracy.

21 JANUARY 1941 : ITALIAN CRUISER FIRED IN TOBRUK HARBOUR. The cruiser "San Giorgio," damaged earlier in the month by the R.A.F. and beached in Tobruk Harbour, where she was used as a fortress mounting anti-aircraft guns, was set on fire from the air on 21 January. The picture shows her last moments as she burns furiously amidships.

CAPTURE OF TOBRUK. The final assault on Tobruk was launched at dawn on 21 January, and its capture was completed by nightfall on 22 January. The attack, which was strongly assisted by naval and air forces, was led by Australian troops, who once more distinguished themselves by their rapid penetration of the outer

defences and their courage and dash in the final assault.   Free French troops also played an important part in
the attack.   The picture above, specially drawn for this book by T. C. Dugdale, A.R.A., depicts the final assault
on the town by Australians with tanks in support, while British air and naval units bombard the town.

ASSAULT ON TOBRUK. The battle of Tobruk followed the lines of that at Bardia, the town being attacked simultaneously from several points. By skilfully encircling the enemy positions the attackers were able to take Italian forces in the rear, thereby throwing them into confusion and making them face both ways at once. Allied casualties were very light, less than 500 in all; nearly 20,000 Italian prisoners were taken as well as

many guns and large stores of material. Above, left, a British medium howitzer in action during the preliminary bombardment. Right, British infantry making their way through barbed wire defences outside the town. Below, men of the Australian Imperial forces advancing towards their objective supported by light tanks. They are disposed in open formation as a precaution against bombing from the air.

HAILE SELASSIE AT HOME AGAIN. The British successes against the Italians in Abyssinia encouraged the Ethiopians to revolt. When Ras Mongasha raised the Imperial Standard at Gojjam in July, 1940, large numbers of the patriots rallied to the call. A British mission had kept in close contact with the patriots, and the Emperor, Haile Selassie, established in Khartoum, had visited his troops at the frontier at the end of the previous year. On 15 January he flew into the heart of Abyssinia, where he unfurled his standard (above) on his native soil, from which he had been absent since May, 1937. In the lower picture he is seen stepping from his plane at a secret landing ground.

Roosevelt welcomes Lord Halifax

NEW BRITISH AMBASSADOR IN AMERICA. The death of Lord Lothian, Britain's representative, in Washington, on 12 December, 1940, left a diplomatic gap which was filled a fortnight later by the appointment of Lord Halifax. The selection of so prominent a statesman as Ambassador was unprecedented, and was received with deep satisfaction in the United States. Lord Halifax, who crossed to America in the battleship "King George V," was met in Chesapeake Bay by President Roosevelt, who journeyed from Washington specially to welcome him. Above, the President and the new Ambassador are seen together shortly after the latter's arrival.

29 JANUARY, 1941: DERNA CAPTURED. Derna, the next objective on the Libyan coast after Tobruk for General Wavell's troops, was captured by the Australians and British on 29 January after three days' fighting. Though their strength had been sapped at Bardia and Tobruk, the Italians defended this vital water depot with great tenacity. The picture shows British artillery pounding at the defences of the town.

BRITISH SUCCESS IN ERITREA. On 1 February, the Anglo-Indian forces, with R.A.F. support, captured Agordat, capital of western Eritrea. The enemy suffered heavy casualties and lost a number of tanks and guns. This success cleared the road to Keren, on which town was based the defence of Asmara, the Eritrean capital, and the Red Sea port of Massawa. The pictures show : above, Indians with a Bren gun carrier clearing an Eritrean village ; below, British soldiers with Bren guns and rifles sniping at the enemy from behind the rocks.

Benghazi gives in without a fight

BRITISH IN CYRENAICA'S CAPITAL. The army of the Nile crowned its two months' campaign on 6 February by occupying Benghazi, the capital of eastern Libya. The resistance encountered here was small, for after a British mechanized force had cut the town's communications in the south, the enemy gave up without a fight. Above, Italian and native residents watch the ceremony of handing over the town to the victors; below, inhabitants give the Australian troops a warm welcome as they march into the town.

W.I.P.2—F*

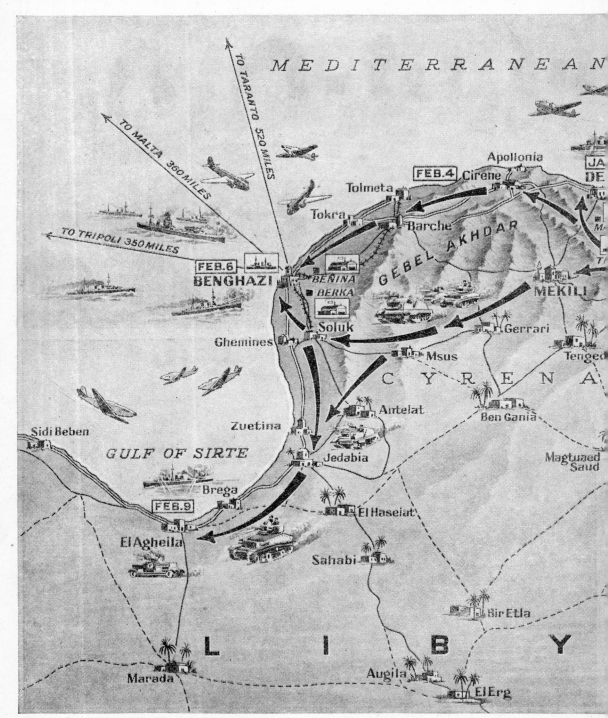

BRITAIN'S CONQUEST OF EASTERN LIBYA. The brilliant forward movement along the coast of Italian North Africa, begun on 9 December, 1940, and culminating in the capture of Benghazi on 6 February, 1941, was acclaimed as one of the most brilliant campaigns in military history. The army of the Nile, consisting of about 30,000 men, advanced within two months over 500 miles through practically roadless and waterless country, with ever-lengthening lines of communication. They captured about 140,000 prisoners, including

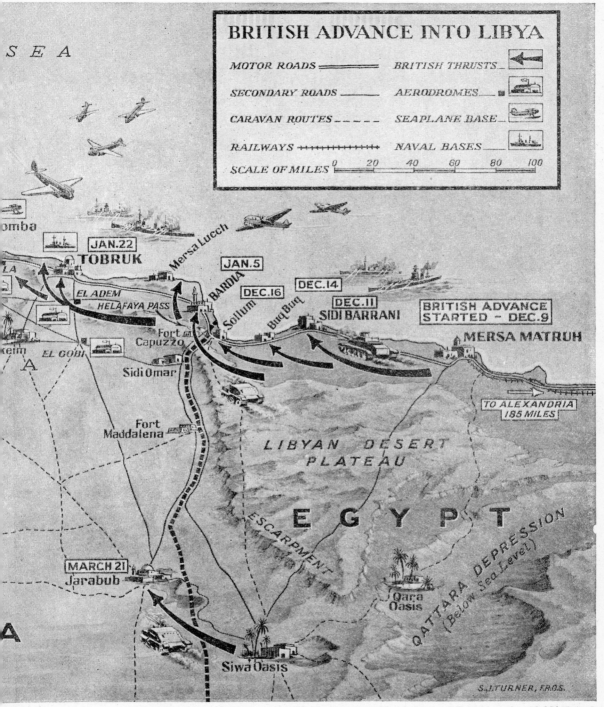

BRITISH ADVANCE INTO LIBYA

MOTOR ROADS ════════	BRITISH THRUSTS
SECONDARY ROADS ────────	AERODROMES
CARAVAN ROUTES ─ ─ ─ ─	SEAPLANE BASE
RAILWAYS ++++++++++++++	NAVAL BASES

SCALE OF MILES   0   20   40   60   80   100

S E A

omba

JAN. 22
TOBRUK

Mersa Lueeh

EL ADEM
HELÁFAYA PASS

JAN. 5
BARDIA

Soilum

DEC. 16

Buq Buq

DEC. 14

DEC. 11
SIDI BARRANI

Fort
Capuzzo

El GOBI

Sidi Omar

BRITISH ADVANCE
STARTED – DEC. 9

MERSA MATRUH

LA

eim

A

Fort
Maddalena

LIBYAN   DESERT
PLATEAU

TO ALEXANDRIA
185 MILES

E   G   Y   P   T

ESCARPMENT

QATTARA DEPRESSION
(Below Sea Level)

Qara
Oasis

MARCH 21
Jarabub

A

Siwa Oasis

S. J. TURNER, F.R.G.S.

nineteen enemy generals, with vast quantities of war material of all kinds, at a cost of only about 2,000 British casualties. During the earlier stages great assistance was given to the land army by naval supporting forces, and the success was also due in great measure to the air superiority early established by the R.A.F. The map above shows pictorially the stages of the advance, indicating the final move on Benghazi by Australian troops using the coastal road and British armoured units cutting Italian communications from the south.

NAVY POUNDS ITALIAN NAVAL BASE. In an early morning bombardment of Genoa by the Mediterranean Fleet on 9 February more than three hundred tons of shells were rained on the harbour. Many important objectives, including the main power station, the Ansaldo electrical and boiler works, the oil fuel installations, and several supply ships, were repeatedly hit by heavy shells. Above, a view of the harbour at Genoa; below, the British battleship "Renown," which took part in the bombardment, carrying out heavy gunnery practice.

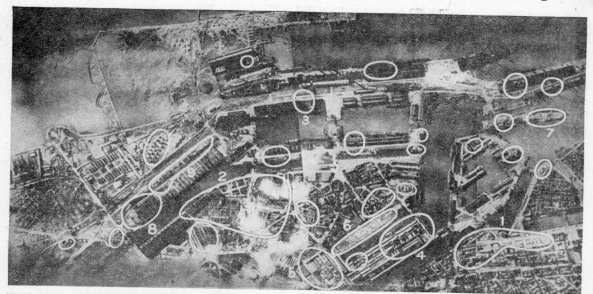

FRENCH AND BELGIAN PORTS BOMBED. During the winter the R.A.F. attacks on the "invasion ports" continued, and, with the approach of spring, were redoubled. The accuracy of the British bombing is well illustrated by the above photographs taken by reconnaissance planes shortly afterwards. They show (above), damage at Le Havre : 1, Kleber Barracks ; 2 to 8, partially or completely destroyed warehouses and other buildings on the quays ; 9, sheds by the Harbour Railway Station ; below, docks at Ostend, showing destroyed warehouses.

NEW BRITISH AIR ARM IN ACTION. On the night of 10–11 February British parachute detachments landed in Calabria, South Italy, to demolish port objectives in the neighbourhood. Though a number were captured,

the temporary suspension of traffic on the South Italian railways was announced a few days later. The picture, by M. Mackinlay, shows the troops landing near an aqueduct whose destruction was one of their objectives.

BRITAIN'S AIRBORNE TROOPS. The training of Britain's new arm, the parachute troops, was undertaken by the Army and the R.A.F. in collaboration, at a secret R.A.F. station in Great Britain. On the left are seen some of the parachutists in the second stage of their training. They are jumping from a dummy fuselage; counter-balance weights regulate the speed of their fall, making it equivalent to that which would be attained in an actual jump. Above, troops jumping from their planes; and, below, the descent as the parachutes open.

BRITISH VICTORIES IN ITALIAN SOMALILAND. The South African and Gold Coast troops advancing into Italian Somaliland occupied on 11 February the military centre of Afmadu, and on 15th captured the port of Kismayu, the Royal Navy co-operating with the attackers. Jumbo was taken on 23rd, and the way opened to the capital, Mogadishu, which fell on 25th. Some of the Italian native troops who were taken prisoner are shown above, left; top, right, a British doctor examines a wounded prisoner. Below, left, some of the guns and transport cap.ured from the Italians; right, inhabitants of Mogadishu, under the shadow of the fasces, watch with interest naval vessels off the town.

Britain's women play their p

THE WOMEN GO TO IT. As the armed forces and war industries absorbed additional men, more and more women came forward to fill their places. Top left, a girl mechanic is at work on machine gun parts;

centre, women training to be bus conductors; right, women porters at a railway goods yard; bottom left, Britain's first women signallers learning the job; right, girls loading a mail train at a London terminus.

BULGARIA ACCEPTS "NEW ORDER." Bulgaria had frequently reiterated her intention of maintaining neutrality, but at the end of February it became obvious that the pretence was wearing thin, and on 1 March the Premier, Prof. Filoff, flew to Vienna and there (top right) signed a pact with the Axis in Hitler's presence. Filoff is seated left, with Ribbentrop (centre) and Count Ciano (right).   Top, left, German "Stuka" dive bombers flying over Sofia, as hints that quick signature would be advisable; below, left, German tanks enter Bulgaria, which the Nazis had already begun to occupy as the pact was being signed; right, Nazi tanks in Sofia.

NEW AMERICAN AMBASSADOR IN BRITAIN. On 10 February it was announced that Mr. J. G. Winant, a close friend of the President, would succeed Mr. J. P. Kennedy as American Ambassador to Britain. Mr. Winant arrived in England on 1 March and was welcomed on his way to London (above) by the King. Below, Mr. Churchill, Mr. Winant, Lord Cranborne (Dominions Secretary) and Lord Moyne (Colonial Secretary) signing the agreement providing for the lease of air and naval bases in British Atlantic possessions to America.

BRILLIANT ALLIED RAID ON NORWAY. On 4 March British troops and light naval forces, aided by Norwegian marines, carried out a raid on the Lofoten Islands, near Narvik. They destroyed the fish-oil production plant, sank eleven enemy ships, took a number of prisoners, brought off about 300 Norwegian patriots, and left supplies for the local population. Little opposition was encountered, and no casualties suffered. The picture shows a motor landing craft with troops aboard, making for the shore to effect the landing.

4 MARCH, 1941: GERMAN OIL PLANT DESTROYED. Here the oil storage wells at Stansund are seen ablaze after they have been fired by the landing party. The British troops in the foreground are guarding the wells while their comrades round up the "Quislings" and German personnel.

RESULTS OF THE LOFOTEN RAID.   The raid on the Lofotens took the Nazis completely by surprise.   The attackers me⁺ with practically no opposition, and suffered no casualties, though a few German sailors were killed.   Above, German merchant seamen and air ground staff and Norwegian "quislings" being transferred, blindfolded, from one ship to another on the way to Britain; below, one of the landing craft leaving after the raid loaded with troops and recruits for the Free Norwegian forces; top, right, British troops return to their ship, leaving smoking oil tanks behind them; below, dense clouds of smoke rising from the burning oil tanks.

YET MORE AMERICAN AID. On 10 January, President Roosevelt introduced in Congress a "Lease and Lend Bill" providing for authority to be given to the U.S. Government to manufacture "defence articles" of all kinds and to "sell, lease, lend, or otherwise dispose of" them to the Allied Governments. After hot debates in Congress the Bill became law on 11 March. Above, Mr. Wendell Willkie, giving evidence on the Bill before the Senate Foreign Relations Committee; below, Mr. Roosevelt, signing the Bill at the White House.

BRITAIN'S GIRL SOLDIERS AT WORK. The Auxiliary Territorial Service, formed some months before the war began, was now performing duties of the first importance in connexion with home defence, especially in anti-aircraft operations. Above, A.T.S. girls at a training post for anti-aircraft gunners; while the gunners fire at a target, the girls on the left, photograph the shell-bursts with a kine-theodolite, while those at the table map the hits; below, women in battle dress double to action stations at an A.A. post, where they operate predictors.

NAZI BOMBERS OVER THE PROVINCES. The main attack of the Luftwaffe was now being directed against the large industrial cities of the provinces, especially the ports and coastal towns. Heavy raids on Merseyside took place on 12 and 13 March, the damage being mainly confined to private houses, though schools, a hospital, and industrial premises were also hit. The first heavy attack on Clydeside came on 13 March, and was resumed

on the following night, blocks of flats and tenement houses being the chief sufferers. Thirteen enemy bombers —a record number so far—were destroyed on the night of 13 March. Left, bombed-out Clydesiders take their rescued belongings to temporary shelter; right, above, homeless women and children in a Liverpool street after a night raid; below, Merseyside rescue workers searching the wreckage for victims immediately after a raid.

U.S. SQUADRON AT SYDNEY. In March a U.S. naval squadron comprising two cruisers and five destroyers paid a visit to Australia and New Zealand. It was commanded by Admiral Newton who, at a dinner given by the Commonwealth Government to himself and his officers, declared that the U.S. was behind Britain and her dominions in their great fight for freedom. American sailors and marines who marched through Sydney followed

by detachments of militia and the Royal Australian Air Force, received a tremendous welcome from the people of the city. The previous visit by U.S. warships to Australian waters had been made in June, 1926, when the American squadron was led by the flagship "Theodore Roosevelt." The picture above shows launches and other small craft escorting the American warships down Sydney harbour as they sailed for Brisbane.

195

DEVASTATION BY LUFTWAFFE AT PLYMOUTH. Nazi bombers made Plymouth their main target in two particularly heavy night raids towards the end of March. The destruction wrought by the attacks was officially stated to be at least as heavy as any provincial city had so far sustained in air attacks. The "military objectives" hit included, as usual, dwelling houses, shops, churches, schools, cinemas and hotels, and the casualties were heavy. In the second raid, the more severe of the two, more than 20,000 incendiary bombs were dropped, in

addition to hundreds of high explosives. These were followed by sustained dive bombing and machine gun attacks on the blazing ruins, but on both nights the serious fires started were soon brought under control by the local fire-fighting services who stayed at their posts in spite of the ferocity of the bombardment. Mr. Menzies, the Australian Premier, who was in the city at the time, helped in rescue work. Left, one of the bombed areas of a business district; right, Mr. Churchill is welcomed as he tours the city after the raids.

Jarabub surrenders after

ITALIAN DESERT GARRISON CAPTURED. Jarabub, an isolated town in the Libyan desert, about 250 miles south of Tobruk, and the burial place of the founder of the Senussi sect of Mohammedans, was captured by British and Imperial troops on 21 March after a siege lasting fifteen weeks. The pictures show: top, left,

Australians with fixed bayonets searching the citadel for Italian troops who may be in hiding; below, left, the inhabitants watching an Australian battalion parading for roll call after the battle; right, Australian soldiers beside the prostrate bodies of two of the many Italian soldiers who perished during the final assault.

NAZIS TO ITALY'S AID.   The farthest point on the Libyan coast reached by Wavell's army was El Agheila, 175 miles west of Benghazi.   On 24 March it was announced that this small town had been re-occupied by an enemy force believed to include German armoured units.   It later transpired that the Germans had succeeded in shipping "panzer" units to Africa to bolster up the morale of the Italians.   Above, German soldiers are unloading guns from a transport plane and, below, a German "Stork" plane, just landed from a transport.

ERITREAN MOUNTAIN FASTNESS CAPTURED. Keren, Italian key fortress in Eritrea, defended by some 60,000 men, a third of the Italian forces in E. Africa, fell to the British on 26 March. In the capture of the heights that surround the town Indian troops, fighting against tremendous odds, played a magnificent part. The pictures show: top, aircrews who took part in the bombing of the town being shown their objectives on a scale model of the battle area; below, an Indian observation post on one of the mountains close to the town.

GERMAN PLAN FOR BALKANS FOILED. In mid-March Germany demanded that Yugoslavia should align itself with the Axis powers, and on the 25th the Premier, M. Tsvetkovich, signed at Vienna a treaty by which Yugoslavia adhered to the Tripartite Pact. The news was received with consternation in the country, and at midnight on the 26th a revolution broke out, led by General Simovich, who became Premier. Above, M. Tsvetkovich (centre) and his foreign minister, M. Cincar-Markovich (left) take leave of Ribbentrop at Salzburg after a conference with Hitler in February; below, students demonstrating in a Belgrade street after the coup d'état.

GREAT BRITISH NAVAL VICTORY. The battle of Cape Matapan, described fully on pages 204 and 205, considerably altered the balance of naval power in the Mediterranean. Three of Italy's heaviest cruisers, "Pola," "Fiume" and "Zara," and two large destroyers were sunk. The above pictures show aspects of the first stage of the battle: top, H.M. destroyer "Hasty" steaming past enemy shells bursting near her; centre, destroyers laying a smoke screen to protect the British ships from the fire of the Italian battleship, "Vittorio Veneto," which was later badly damaged; bottom, H.M.S. "Gloucester" laying a smoke screen early in the battle.

ITALY'S CRUSHING DEFEAT. On 27 March reconnaissance planes reported the presence of the Italian battleship "Vittorio Veneto," with eight cruisers and nine destroyers, off Sicily. The Mediterranean Fleet immediately put to sea and joined action. On being attacked by British torpedoes the "Vittorio Veneto" headed off towards her base. She was pursued by the British ships which, in the afternoon, met a second enemy fleet of two battleships, three cruisers and four destroyers. Fleet Air Arm craft scored several hits on the Italian

ships, and at night the Imperial forces, consisting of three battleships, an aircraft carrier, four cruisers and a number of destroyers, engaged the Italian armada of three battleships, eleven cruisers and fourteen destroyers, with the result already recorded. The engagement resulted in no British casualties to ships or men. The picture above, specially drawn for this book by Stanley Rogers, shows the British flagship "Warspite" hurling at the "Fiume" from the close range of 4,000 yards the rain of shells which sent her to the bottom.

GERMANS BOMB ITALIAN SAILORS. It was estimated that 3,000 Italian officers and men, including an admiral, perished n the Matapan engagement. British ships picked up over 900 survivors as well as thirty-five German naval officers and ratings, and the number of men so rescued would have been much larger had not German dive bombing attacks compelled the rescue work to be abandoned. Admiral Cunningham, the British commander, then signalled the position of the unrescued Italians to their own naval authorities so that a hospital ship could be sent. The picture above shows three rafts with Italian sailors waiting to be rescued.

Atlantic raider meets its doom

FATE OF GERMAN U-BOATS. With the approach of spring the Nazi campaign against British and Allied shipping was greatly intensified, and in March the total losses, British, Allied, and neutral, amounted to 119 ships, with a total tonnage of 489,229 tons. German battle cruisers as well as U-boats were reported to be operating in the Atlantic, but measures against the raiders were intensified too, and the certain destruction of three U-boats was announced during the month. The upper picture shows the last member of a destroyed U-boat's crew about to jump from the vessel; below, the crew in the water after abandoning ship.

BATTLE OF THE ATLANTIC. Hitler's boast that, with the coming of the spring, German U-boat and aerial war against Britain's convoys in the Atlantic would be intensified was no idle one. In March and April British and Allied losses rose to 489,229 and 488,124 tons respectively, representing in all 225 ships. In spite of all

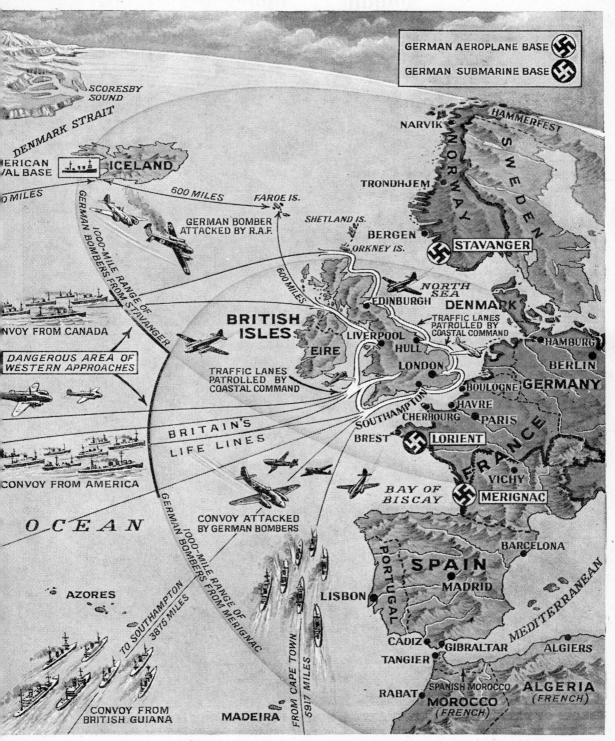

the enemy could do, however, Britain's lifeline, though stretched, remained unbroken thanks to the fine work of the Navy and Royal Air Force. The map above shows the routes taken by the convoys and the measures taken to outwit the enemy submarines and long-range bombers operating from Lorient, Stavanger and Merignac.

HEROES OF BATTLE OF THE ATLANTIC. As Hitler had threatened, Nazi efforts to cut Britain's lifelines reached their climax in the spring. In spite of heavy losses from U-boats and sur.ace raiders, food and munitions still poured into Britain, and nothing could prevent the Red Ensign from floating as proudly as ever on the world's seas. The pictures show: top, fast motor launches guarding a convoy as it steams down the English Channel; below, the look-out of an attendant destroyer scans the sea for possible enemy submarines.

MEN WHO COMMAND THE U-BOATS. The Admiralty announced in May that, although many U-boats had been destroyed leaving no survivors, about 500 officers and ratings from sunken German submarines had been made prisoners. Among them was Commander Otto Kretschmer, U-boat ace, decorated by Hitler in August, 1940. Another famed commander, Captain Schepke, went down with U-100 in mid-April. The picture shows Captain Schutze, another Nazi hero of the submarine war, saying farewell before leaving for a raiding cruise.

ERITREAN CAPITAL OCCUPIED. On 1 April the British forces advancing after their victory at Keren accepted the surrender of Asmara, capital of Italy's oldest colony, a city of 100,000 people. It had been declared an open town by the Italians, and the defending forces withdrew to new positions to the south of the city. The upper picture shows Imperial troops and Bren gun carriers marching through the city; below, some of the Indian troops who had played such a great and gallant part in the advance are seen entering the town.

ALLIED LEADERS IN THE MIDDLE EAST.   The resumption of activity in Libya brought about by German reinforcements created a difficult situation for the middle eastern command, for the expected attack on Greece made it imperative that troops should be withdrawn from the African front.   As a result British and Free French commanders met in Cairo to discuss the situation. Above they are in conversation. Left to right, General Wavell, General de Gaulle, General Catroux, Major-General E. L. Spears, and Air Chief Marshal Sir A. Longmore.

213

NAZIS ADVANCE IN LIBYA. The withdrawal of large numbers of British troops from Cyrenaica enabled the German division that had come to Italy's aid in the previous month to push the slender British forces back. On 3 April the enemy entered Benghazi, but the British were able to destroy all the war material they had previously captured from the Italians. The pictures show the advance of a Nazi "panzer" division along the coastal road in Cyrenaica. The natives in the lower picture would appear to be accustomed to the sight of tanks.

MERCHANT SHIPS SCUTTLED IN AMERICA. After acts of sabotage by the crews of Italian merchant ships in U.S.A. harbours, the government decided to place Axis vessels in "protective custody." This example was followed a few days later by other American republics. When the Italian S.S. "Felia" (top, left) and the German "Eisenach" (top, right) were set on fire at Puntarenas, the Costa Rica Government charged their crews with arson. Below, Italian seamen from the liner "Conte Biancamano" being taken into custody at Ellis Island.

ABYSSINIAN CAPITAL RECOVERED. On the evening of 5 April, South African troops, after an advance of 700 miles in the short space of twenty-seven days, entered Addis Ababa, thus wrested from Italian hands after an occupation lasting since 1936. The city was surrendered by the Italians without any attempt at resistance; the Italian Viceroy, the Duke of Aosta, and part of the garrison had already withdrawn. In the picture a well-

known Transvaal regiment, headed by its pipers, is seen marching through the liberated town accompanied by delighted Abyssinians who after five years under the Fascist yoke, have been freed from virtual slavery. A month later, on 5 May, the fifth anniversary of the entry of the Italian troops into the capital, the Emperor, Haile Selassie, returned to his capital in triumph and was greeted by all his religious and military leaders.

ANOTHER VICTIM OF NAZI AGGRESSION. Germany's anger at the coup d'état which had spoiled her plans in Yugoslavia at once reached fever pitch. A campaign o abuse began in the German press, "atrocities" against German residents in Yugoslavia were alleged, and German consular officials were called home. On 6 April, without declaration of war or previous warning, Germany invaded Yugoslavia and Greece. Aid from Britain and America to the invaded countries was immediately promised, but the new Government in Belgrade had had no time to make preparations against attack, and the country was quickly overrun. The pictures show: top, left, tank traps being pushed aside by German tanks during the march in; right, uprooted rail tracks after a bombing raid; below, left, Yugoslav infantrymen waiting for the invader; right, light tanks, lorries and motor cycle combinations of a German "panzer" division moving into Yugoslavia.

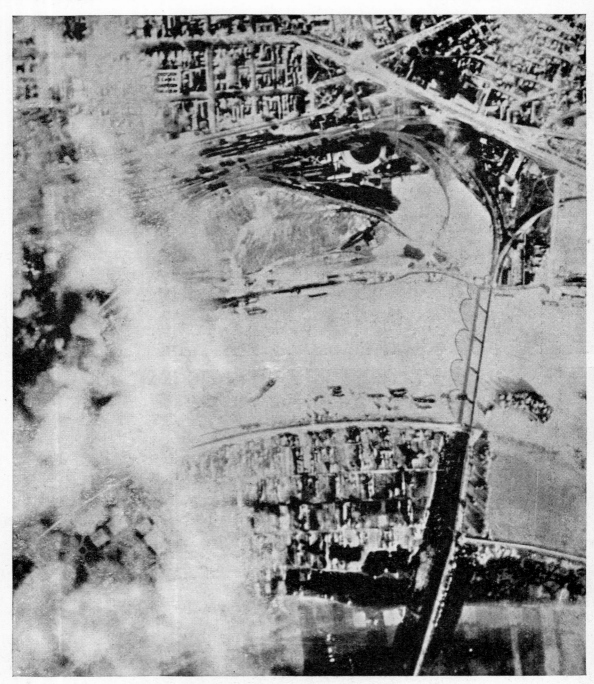

RUTHLESS ATTACK ON YUGOSLAV CAPITAL. The German onslaught on Yugoslavia opened with a savage bombing raid on Belgrade in the morning of 6 April, in spite of the fact that the capital had been declared an open city. Three further attacks took place during the day, rivalling in ferocity the earlier raids on Warsaw and Rotterdam. Although the small Yugoslav air force gallantly attacked the numerically superior enemy formations, thousands of civilians were killed, and much of the city laid in ruins. Above, an aerial view of part of the city just after the first raid, showing fires raging in several quarters. Right, Nazi tanks passing General von Kleist in front of the Yugoslav Parliament Building after the occupation of the city on 12 April.

FIRST DAY OF BALKAN ADVANCE. Germany began the attack on Greece by an advance through the Rupel Pass into the Struma Valley, leading from Bulgaria into Greece, with a view to the capture of Salonika and the cutting off of the Greek troops in eastern Thrace from their main body. The pictures show various aspects of the advance: top, left, a Nazi motorized unit protected by anti-aircraft guns against surprise attack

from the air, pressing on through the rough Balkan countryside on their way to the Greek frontier; below, German artillerymen hauling an 8·8 cm. gun across a pontoon bridge hastily erected over a Balkan river; right, a German tank ablaze after it has received a direct hit from Greek artillery. The trailer ropes at the left of the picture show that it was aiding another damaged vehicle when it was itself destroyed.

GERMANS OCCUPY ÆGEAN PORTS. German armoured divisions captured Dedeagach on 7 April, thus cutting off Greece from Turkey, and on the following day the rapid advance down the Vardar Valley after the Yugoslavs had withdrawn from southern Serbia enabled the Nazis to occupy Salonika. Greek and British troops had destroyed the port installations before the German occupation. The picture shows German anti-tank gunners who took part in the Balkan operations in action against the Greek mechanized units.

BOMB DAMAGE IN GERMAN CAPITAL. On the night of 9 April British airmen made the heaviest attack on Berlin which the city had so far suffered. Neutral reports said that terrific damage was done, especially in the Government quarter and that civilian casualties amounted to over 2,000. The State Opera House, from which flames are seen pouring in the picture above, Prussian State Library, Bellevue Palace, and the New Palace at Potsdam, suffered severely from the effects of the heavy high-explosive bombs that were used.

W.I.P.2—H

HUNGARIANS BREAK TREATY OF FRIENDSHIP. In February Hungary signed a pact of eternal friendship with Yugoslavia: the lower picture shows the Hungarian and Yugoslav Foreign Ministers, MM. Bardossy (left) and Cincar-Markovich (centre) reviewing a guard of honour on this occasion in Budapest. But on 11 April Hungarian troops invaded the Banat, which had been Hungarian territory before 1918. In the upper picture a brigade of Hungarian motorized troops that took part in the invasion is seen passing through Budapest.

INTENSE AIR ATTACK ON CAPITAL. On the night of 16 April a force of over 500 German bombers attacked London in what was estimated to be its most destructive raid of the war up to that date. Most of the damage done was by fire, the Nazis claiming that over 100,000 incendiary bombs were dropped. As usual, hospitals, churches, private residences and other non-military objectives suffered most severely. This photograph of a blazing city building was taken at the height of the "Blitz."

**HEAVY NIGHT RAIDS DES-
TROY MORE CHURCHES.**
Churches were among the
principal sufferers in the
heavy raid on London of 16
April, and the almost equally
heavy raid three nights later.
These raids were announced
in Germany as reprisals for
the successful R.A.F. raid on
Berlin on the night of 9-10
April. In the attack of the 16th,
six enemy bombers were
shot down—three by A.A.
fire and three by night-
fighters, bringing the month's
total to sixty-five and the
year's to 142. Widespread
raids over provincial towns
also took place during April,
especially at Belfast on the
15th and Portsmouth on the
17th. The pictures show: top,
left, St. Mildred's, Bread
Street, London, a Wren
church which has been called
"a miniature Essay for St.
Paul's"; centre, a Belfast
Presbyterian church fired by
incendiary bombs; right, the

gutted shell of St. Clement Danes, one of Wren's most beautiful creations, its charred and bare walls still standing on its island site in the Strand roadway. This famous church had been damaged in previous raids. Bottom, left, the results of a further hit on St. Paul's Cathedral, where a gaping hole in the floor of the north transept was caused by a bomb falling through the roof. Several incendiary bombs fell on to the roof but were quickly extinguished by the A.R.P. workers. Centre, the rubble where once stood the seven hundred-year-old parish church of Bromley, Kent, destroyed, save for its tower, by a direct hit; right, what the Nazis left of the Roman Catholic Cathedral of St. George, Southwark. Other buildings damaged in the raid of the 16th were Guy's Hospital, St. Andrew's, Holborn and the City Temple.

ANOTHER AXIS CONQUEST. Although the Yugoslav troops put up a brave resistance to the invaders, their position was hopeless from the beginning, for the government that had been in power before the coup d'état of 27 March had done nothing to prepare the country for the struggle. On 16 April Sarajevo was captured, and the Yugoslav army capitulated on 17 April. The upper picture shows Yugoslav troops with the white flag of surrender, after the capitulation, marching under escort down a road lined with German tanks; below, a blockhouse, fired by defenders when further resistance was impossible, is occupied by German troops.

GREEK RESISTANCE NEARS ITS END. The occupation of Yugoslavia and the consequent release of German troops rendered critical the position of the Greek armies that had gallantly harried the Italians in southern Albania. A strongly mechanized German thrust to their rear near Yanina soon cut them off from the main Greek army farther south; their anti-tank equipment was negligible, and in spite of the desperate resistance of small isolated groups such as that shown in the lower picture, they failed to stem the German advance. Above, Nazi troops, covered by machine gunners, are operating against the Greeks with portable flame-throwers.

EPIRUS FORCES SURROUNDED. The German advance from Monastir besides separating the Greeks in Epirus from their comrades to the South, enabled the German and Italian troops to join forces. The picture

shows an Italian artilleryman firing a medium gun at the crumbling Greek concentrations behind the front line in Albania shortly before the gallant Greek Army was forced to surrender to the combined Axis forces.

END OF A BRAVE STRUGGLE. The Greek army of Epirus and Macedonia surrendered at Larissa on the afternoon of 22 April, after a heroic fight against greatly superior German and Italian forces, and signed an armistice with the Italian commander; on the same day the Greek king and government left the mainland for Crete. Top, General Tsolakoglu signs the armistice documents placed before him by German staff officers; below, Greek soldiers of the Epirot army with an out-of-date field-piece, typical of the weapons with which they had for so long held the Italians at bay, but which availed little against the superior equipment of the Nazis.

GERMANS ATTACK DESERT GARRISON. Although the British were obliged to abandon most of the territory they had captured in Libya, they managed to hold the strategically important town of Tobruk. Supplied with food and munitions by sea, the garrison beat off repeated enemy attacks in one of which, on 25 April, they captured two officers and 125 men, besides killing and wounding many others. These pictures, taken inside the Tobruk defences, show, above, an A.A. gun team, behind a barricade of munition boxes, on the watch for Nazi bombers; below, a British transport unloading food and munitions for the defending forces.

NAZI GRIP ON GREECE TIGHTENS. The Anglo-Greek forces were compelled to fall back as heavy reinforcements of German troops and machines, supported by dive bombers in vast numbers, poured into northern Greece. Whole regiments of Nazis were mown down in rearguard actions as the British and Greeks withdrew to shorter defence lines. On 25 April the famous pass of Thermopylae was taken after a heroic resistance

by Anzac troops; on the same day German troops occupied Lemnos and other Greek islands; on 26 April they took Thebes, and on the 27th parachute troops occupied the town and isthmus of Corinth. The pictures show: top, a caique hauling boat-loads of Nazis from the Greek mainland to occupy the island of Eubœa; below, left, German motor cyclists passing through Corinth streets; and right, Nazi paratroops in action in Corinth.

NAZIS IN GREEK CAPITAL. Though Athens itself was not the victim of air attack by the Germans, possibly in view of the R.A.F.'s warning that such an exploit would be followed by the bombing of Rome, its suburbs were a target for the Luftwaffe on 22 and 25 April. The occupation of the capital on 27 April was celebrated by a great parade of German and Italian troops. Left, German (above) and Italian (below) motorized detachments saluting General List. Right, German infantry marching down a main street with the Acropolis in the background.

Charles Cundall

IMPERIAL FORCES LEAVE GREECE. A statement by Australia's acting premier had prepared the Empire for the news that the British troops, in view of the overwhelming German onslaught, were to withdraw from Greece; and on 30 April Mr. Eden, Foreign Minister, announced that the withdrawal had been urged by the Greek Government to prevent further vain sacrifices. The story of the evacuation was told on 3 May. It was

undertaken at night under severe dive-bombing and in face of heavy air superiority. Of some 55,000 Anzacs and British troops, over three-quarters were got away safely, with all their light equipment: two destroyers were lost during the operations. This picture, specially drawn by Charles Cundall, A.R.A., shows the last phase of the evacuation from southern Greece. Troops are being taken to the destroyers in Greek caiques.

241

HEROES OF THE GREEK WITHDRAWAL BACK IN AFRICA. The British and Imperial troops operating in Greece were nearly all seasoned veterans of the campaigns in Africa. They had been mainly drawn from the Army of the Nile, and on their evacuation returned to Egypt. The picture above shows

a transport-load of Anzac and British tommies who have just landed at an Egyptian port after their heroic rearguard fight and hazardous crossing of the Mediterranean. They are taking a well-earned rest on the quayside, and appear to be little affected by the gruelling experiences they have just undergone.

243

AIR FORCE HELP IN GREEK WITHDRAWAL. Magnificent work was done during the Greek evacuation by the R.A.F.'s flying boats, which picked up heavy loads of airmen and others from outlying stations from which they could not have reached the embarkation points. One machine took off a load of seventy-two men, fighting off an enemy attack during its journey. Above: R.A.F. personnel being rowed out to a "Sunderland" flying boat; below: R.A.F. ground staff assembling in lorries to be taken to a port in Southern Greece for embarkation.

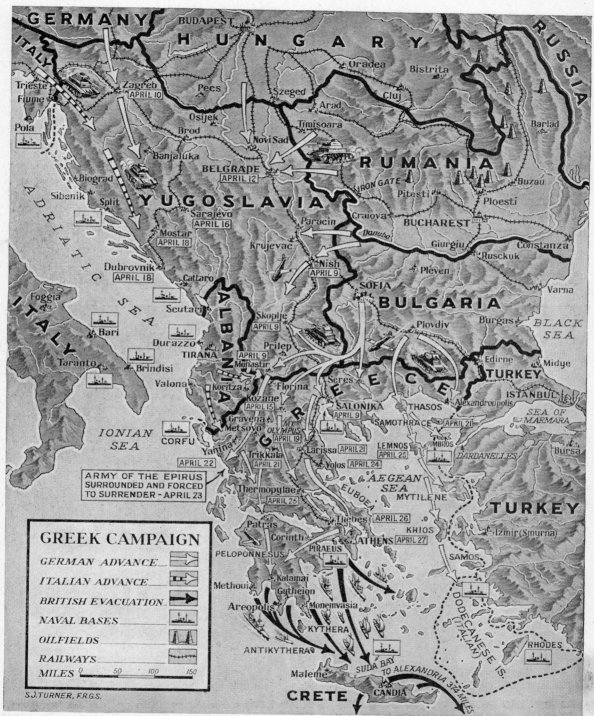

GERMANY

ITALY

Trieste
Fiume
Pola

Zagreb
APRIL 10

BUDAPEST

HUNGARY

Pecs

Osijek

Brod

Banjaluka

Biograd

Sibenik
Split

YUGOSLAVIA

Sarajevo
APRIL 16

Mostar
APRIL 18

Dubrovnik
APRIL 18

Cattaro

ADRIATIC SEA

Scutari

ITALY

Foggia

Bari

Taranto

Durazzo
TIRANA

Brindisi

Valona

ALBANIA

Koritza

Szeged

Arad

Timisoara

Novi Sad

BELGRADE
APRIL 12

Paracin

Krujevac

Nish
APRIL 9

Skoplje
APRIL 9

Prilep
APRIL 9

Monastir
APRIL 9

Florina

Oradea

Cluj

IRON GATE

Pitesti

RUMANIA

Craiova

Danube

BUCHAREST

Giurgiu

Rusckuk

SOFIA

BULGARIA

Plovdiv

Seres

Bistrita

Barlad

Buzau

Ploesti

Constanza

Pleven

Varna

**BLACK
SEA**

Burgas

Edirne

TURKEY

Midye

ISTANBUL

**SEA OF
MARMARA**

Bursa

TURKEY

Kozane
APRIL 15

Gravena
Metsovo

**IONIAN
SEA**

CORFU
APRIL 22

Yanina

Trikkala
APRIL 21

G R E E C E

MT.
OLYMPUS
APRIL 19

Larissa
APRIL 21

Volos
APRIL 24

**ARMY OF THE EPIRUS
SURROUNDED AND FORCED
TO SURRENDER – APRIL 23**

Thermopylae
APRIL 25

SALONIKA
APRIL 9

THASOS

Samothrace

LEMNOS
APRIL 25

IMBROS

Alexandroupolis
APRIL 21

DARDANELLES

**AEGEAN
SEA**

MYTILENE

Izmir (Smyrna)

SAMOS

Patras

Corinth

PELOPONNESUS

Methoui

Kalamai
Gytheion

Areopolis

Monemvasia

KYTHERA

ANTIKYTHERA

Maleme

Tiebes
APRIL 26

ATHENS
APRIL 27

PIRAEUS

EUBOEA

KHIOS

**DODECANESE IS.
(ITALIAN)**

RHODES

SUDA BAY
TO ALEXANDRIA 374 MILES

CRETE

CANDIA

GREEK CAMPAIGN

GERMAN ADVANCE

ITALIAN ADVANCE

BRITISH EVACUATION

NAVAL BASES

OILFIELDS

RAILWAYS

MILES 0   50   100   150

S.J.TURNER, F.R.G.S.

HOW THE NAZIS CAPTURED GREECE. Germany's occupation of Rumania and Bulgaria, and Yugoslavia's refusal to join the Axis, hastened the attack upon Greece. The Germans advanced across the Vardar to Monastir and to Salonika. Yugoslavia was isolated and the Greeks in Albania were threatened. British help could not prevent the Nazis reaching Yanina and forcing the surrender of the Greek Army of the Epirus. The allies were pushed back to the Thermopylae line. The loss of air bases in the Plain of Larissa made the evacuation inevitable.

ANTI-BRITISH MOVEMENT IN IRAQ CRUSHED. On 2 May a clash occurred between British forces and Iraqi troops concentrated round the R.A.F. station at Habbaniyah, near Baghdad. Under the orders of Raschid Ali, the pro-Nazi premier, who had seized power in Iraq a month before, Iraqi troops fired on the aerodrome, destroying British aircraft. The British bombed the rebel troops, and with the assistance of loyal Iraqis expelled them from their positions, at the same time attacking other Iraqi aerodromes where trouble had broken out and destroying a great part of the Iraqi air force. Rutbah, an important air station on the oil line and motor road to

Palestine, which had been occupied by the rebels, was retaken by the British on 10 May after an ultimatum had been dropped by the R.A.F. calling for surrender within an hour. The pictures show: below, left, a cavalry squadron of the Transjordan Arab Legion, recruited almost entirely from Bedouin Arabs, moving out of their camp for patrol duties in the desert; this force assisted the British in their action against the Iraqi rebels. Above, armoured car crew of the Arab Legion's desert patrol. Top, right, armoured car company of the R.A.F. advancing into Iraq after the capture of the fort at Rutbah; below, armoured cars entering the fort after its capture.

REIGN OF TERROR IN POLAND. Speaking to a U.S. audience on 9 May, Lord Halifax, the British Ambassador to Washington, told how the German authorities of the "General Government," the occupied area of Poland, were subjecting the conquered population to a new wave of terror. Over 40,000 Poles, he said, had in all probability been murdered during the few months preceding, and Polish villages were the daily scene of mass floggings and terror reprisals of every kind. These pictures of scenes that were typical of many show: below, left, Polish civilians digging graves for their fellow-countrymen whose bod'es lie beside them; right, the hanging bodies of two Poles who have fallen foul of the occupying forces; above, right, Polish prisoners facing a firing squad; left, a grim procession marched away under Nazi guards to meet a like doom.

LONDON'S SEVEREST AIR RAID. On the full-moon night of 10 May, after an almost raid-free three weeks, London endured an intense air attack lasting for several hours, resulting in many casualties and heavy destruction. Vast numbers of incendiaries were dropped, as well as high explosive bombs, and among the killed were the mayors of two London boroughs. The Houses of Parliament were severely damaged, the Commons' debating chamber being wrecked, but the Commons met the following morning in a building which had been held in

readiness for such an emergency. Westminster Abbey and the British Museum, and many commercial offices and private houses in the City and suburbs, as well as five hospitals, churches, and other public buildings, were hit or burnt out during the raid. Thirty-three enemy planes were brought down—the largest number ever secured in night fighting over England. Left, Mr. Churchill inspects the ruins of a part of the Houses of Parliament; above, a view from Ludgate Circus, looking towards St. Paul's, on the morning after the raid.

MAY RAID DAMAGE IN LONDON. These pictures show some of the results of the great air raid of 10 May. Top, left, the famous bells of St. Clement Danes, Strand, celebrated in nursery rhyme, being moved to safety. The church was reduced to a shell in a previous raid. Centre, firemen at work in Pilgrim Street, close to St. Paul's, on the morrow of the raid. Right, Crown Office Row, in the Temple,

where most of the buildings, including the world-famous round Norman Temple Church, suffered severely. Below, left, results of a bomb that fell in the Central Criminal Court, Old Bailey. Centre, damaged cloisters at Westminster Abbey; right, the wrecked interior of Westminster Upper School, once the monks' dormitory, where the traditional annual ceremony of "tossing the pancake" took place.

British night fighters get the

BRITAIN'S " SECRET WEAPON " PROVES ITS WORTH.   During April night fighters of the R.A.F. began to take serious toll of the German bombers, and by the end of the month they had accounted for fifty out of a record total of eighty-eight destroyed.   These figures, however, were soon to be beaten, and on 4 May thirteen of the enemy fell to their guns.   Three nights later they destroyed a further twenty-four, but on 11 May they broke all records by shooting down a grand total of thirty-three.   The increase in night fighter "kills" was largely due to "Radiolocation," Britain's "secret weapon" which, by the spring of 1941 had reached such a state of perfection that raiding by night became a very risky business for the German bombers.   The pictures show: top, left, W.A.A.F. girls in a subterranean operations room plotting the courses of enemy aircraft on a huge map; bottom, left, night fighter pilots walking to their machines before taking off; right, above, a "Hurricane" night fighter, and, below, a "Blenheim" night fighter about to set off on patrol.

RUDOLF HESS FLIES TO SCOTLAND. The world was astounded to learn on 12 May that Rudolf Hess, Deputy Fuehrer of Germany, had landed near Glasgow by parachute after flying from Germany in a Messerschmitt "110." No official explanation of his desertion was issued, but the general view was that Hess's flight indicated a serious breach of solidarity in the Nazi party, possibly on the question of Russo-German relations. He was treated in Britain as a prisoner of war. Above, Hess, a keen airman, is seen saying good-bye to his wife before taking off on a flight. Below, the wreckage of the machine in which he made his sensational flight.

FRANCO-GERMAN AGREEMENT. On 6 May Admiral Darlan and Herr Abetz, German representative in France, signed an agreement providing for certain "concessions" in the occupation terms, and on 15 May it was announced that the French authorities were allowing German planes to use Syrian airfields. The picture above shows the men of Vichy at a ministerial council. Marshal Pétain, the Premier, is seen on the left of the picture and seated opposite him is Admiral Darlan, the man who negotiated the agreement with the Nazis. Below, the aged Marshal greeted by the crowd during a memorial service to men who fell in the war of 1914-18.

DUKE OF AOSTA SURRENDERS. A culminating point in the East African operations was marked by the surrender on 19 May at Amba Alagi of an Italian army 18,000—19,000 strong. The Duke of Aosta, Viceroy of Abyssinia and Commander-in-Chief of the Italian forces in East Africa, with five generals and a number of his staff officers, was the last to surrender. He is seen in the upper photograph, accompanied by British officers, walking down from the cave which he had used for some time as his headquarters. Below, his defeated forces

The following labels appear on the map:

Port Sudan · Suakin · ARABIA · RED SEA · YEMEN · HADRAMAUT · ADEN · Berber · Atbara · Nile · Atbara · ERITREA · MARCH 26 · KEREN · Agordat · MASSAWA · APRIL 8 · GULF OF ADEN · Bargal · KHARTOUM · Kassala · Biscia · ASMARA · APRIL 1 · Adowa · APRIL 5 · Makale · JUNE 12 · Assab · ADEN · Sennar · Gallabat · Metemma · Gondar · Debra Tabor · AMBA ALAGI · MAY 19 · FRENCH SOMALILAND · JIBUTI · Zeila · BERBERA · MARCH 16 · Kurmuk · Burye · LAKE TANA · Blue Nile · Magdala · Dessye · APRIL 26 · Diredawa · MARCH 29 · BRITISH SOMALILAND · Hargeisa · MARCH 20 · Eil · Asosa · Debra Markos · APRIL 6 · Ankober · Jigiga · MARCH 17 · Harar · ADDIS ABABA · APRIL 5 · Awash · Daggah Bur · MARCH 11 · Burei · Addis Alam · Gambela · ABYSSINIA · Ginir · Wal Wal · Obbia · JIMMA DISTRICT · Allata · Imi · Gorrahei · Scebeli · INDIAN OCEAN · Maji · APRIL 24 · Bako · Neghelli · MARCH 22 · Dolo · Oddur · Fer Fer · ITALIAN SOMALILAND · Yavello · LAKE RUDOLF · Mega · Moyale · FEB. 24 · El Waak · Lugh · Bardera · FEB. 28 · MOGADISHU · FEB. 25 · UGANDA · Soroti · Marsabit · Wajir · Juba · Geleb · Brava · FEB. 24 · KENYA · Archers Post · Afmadu · FEB. 14 · Nanyuki · Garissa · Tana · Kismayu · FEB. 15 · Kisumu · Nakuru · NAIROBI · LAKE VICTORIA · TANGANYIKA

EAST AFRICAN CAMPAIGN

BRITISH THRUSTS	➤
MAIN ROADS	
RAILWAYS	
MILES	0 100 200 300

S.J.TURNER, F.R.G.S.

are accorded the honours of war by the Transvaal Scottish Regiment. The course of the operations in Abyssinia, to which the Prime Minister referred as "a campaign which, I venture to think, is one of the most remarkable ever fought by British or Imperial arms," is indicated on the map on the right. In spite of the difficult country it took the British forces only ninety-four days to cover the 1,500 miles to Amba Alagi. British, Indian and South African troops shared in the operations which were crowned by the Duke's surrender.

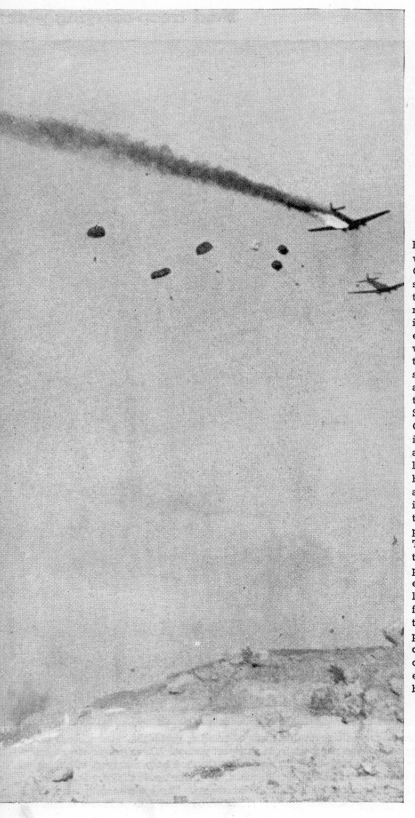

GERMAN AIR-BORNE ATTACK ON CRETE

20 MAY, 1941

Having taken possession of the whole of the Greek mainland, the Germans, on 20 May launched a strong air-borne attack on Crete, the Greek island lying across the mouth of the Ægean Sea. This island was of considerable strategic importance to the enemy who wished to establish air bases there for attacks on British shipping in the Mediterranean and also for possible attempts to establish advance bases in Syria and Iraq. The assault on Crete, launched early in the morning, began with violent bombing attacks, followed by mass troop landings by parachute in the neighbourhood of Maleme and Heraklion aerodromes. Later, gliders towed in "trains" behind bombers, and troop-carrying planes and sea-planes, landed thousands of troops. The Imperial and Greek forces on the island accounted for a high proportion of the invaders, but the enemy threw in their men regardless of cost and gained a firm foothold at Maleme, to the west of the island. The picture shows parachute troops and equipment descending in the neighbourhood of Heraklion airfield; one of the enemy planes is on fire after having been hit by the ground defences.

BATTLE FOR MALEME. The main German attack on Crete was directed against Maleme aerodrome where enemy parachute troops were dropped in large numbers from transport planes. These troops almost immediately gained a foothold and they were able, with the light equipment that had been dropped with them, to beat off Allied attempts to dislodge them. Although the airfield remained under heavy artillery fire for some days the Germans managed to strengthen their hold by further reinforcements. These were mostly transported from the Greek mainland by troop-carrying planes and gliders. The former arrived in a constant stream and

crash-landed on rough country regardless of the huge losses they sustained. The gliders were towed in "trains" behind powerful bombers. They cast themselves off from their parent craft some distance from their objective and glided slowly in to land, if necessary, in very confined spaces. Each glider carried about a dozen soldiers together with enough equipment and stores to make them self-supporting for several days. The picture above, specially drawn by Andrew Johnson, gives a vivid impression of the disembarkation of men and material from the troop-carrying planes at Maleme, under the heavy fire of Allied artillery.

Destruction of troop-carriers

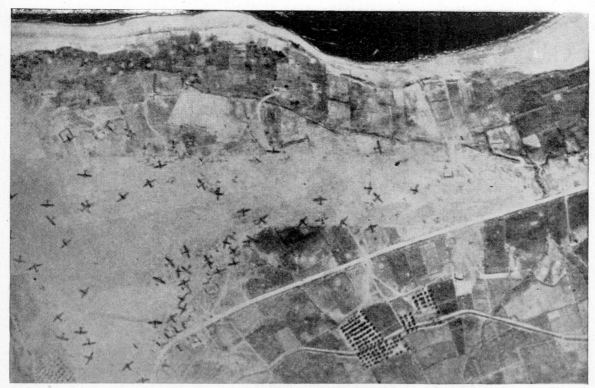

COST OF MALEME CAPTURE. In view of the great disadvantage under which R.A.F. fighters were operating when the attack on Crete was launched, it was decided to withdraw them and leave the defence of the island to land-troops. Unhindered by fighter opposition the enemy were able to land troops in large numbers, and at one period troop-carrying planes at Maleme alone were arriving at the rate of one a minute. Nevertheless enemy casualties were heavy, hundreds of their planes being shot down by the British Fleet lying off the island and by the ground defences. In addition British bombers, escorted by long-range fighters raided the occupied airfields and damaged many enemy planes on the ground. The pictures above, taken by British planes, show the airfield at Maleme strewn with damaged machines. Many of these were wrecked by crash-landings; others were damaged by British bombs. Below, a crashed troop-carrying glider with two of its occupants lying dead beside it.

BRITAIN'S LARGEST BATTLE CRUISER LOST. On 22 May reconnaissance aircraft of the Coastal Command reported that a German battleship and cruiser previously located in Bergen had sailed, and naval forces were at once ordered to intercept them. On the evening of 23 May the enemy were sighted and throughout the night were shadowed by H.M.S. "Norfolk" and "Suffolk." Early the following morning the powerful warships H.M.S. "Prince of Wales" and "Hood" engaged the enemy, and during the action that followed the latter received

loss of H.M.S. "Hood"

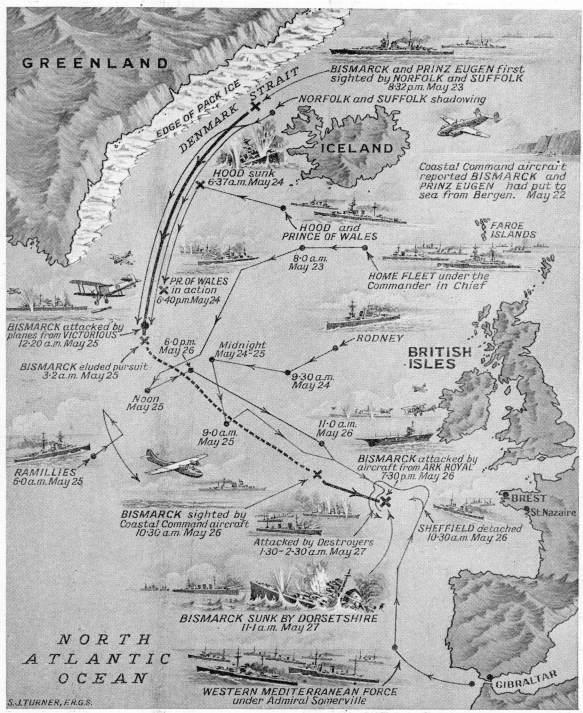

GREENLAND

BISMARCK and PRINZ EUGEN first
sighted by NORFOLK and SUFFOLK
8·32 p.m. May 23

NORFOLK and SUFFOLK shadowing

EDGE OF PACK ICE

DENMARK STRAIT

ICELAND

Coastal Command aircraft
reported BISMARCK and
PRINZ EUGEN had put to
sea from Bergen. May 22

HOOD sunk
6·37 a.m. May 24

HOOD and
PRINCE OF WALES

FAROE
ISLANDS

8·0 a.m.
May 23

HOME FLEET under the
Commander in Chief

PR. OF WALES
in action
6·40 p.m. May 24

BISMARCK attacked by
planes from VICTORIOUS
12·20 a.m. May 25

6·0 p.m.
May 26

Midnight
May 24-25

RODNEY

BISMARCK eluded pursuit
3·2 a.m. May 25

9·30 a.m.
May 24

BRITISH
ISLES

Noon
May 25

9·0 a.m.
May 25

11·0 a.m.
May 26

RAMILLIES
6·0 a.m. May 25

BISMARCK attacked by
aircraft from ARK ROYAL
7·30 p.m. May 26

BREST
St. Nazaire

BISMARCK sighted by
Coastal Command aircraft
10·30 a.m. May 26

SHEFFIELD detached
10·30 a.m. May 26

Attacked by Destroyers
1·30-2·30 a.m. May 27

BISMARCK SUNK BY DORSETSHIRE
11·1 a.m. May 27

N O R T H
A T L A N T I C
O C E A N

S.J.TURNER, F.R.G.S.

GIBRALTAR

WESTERN MEDITERRANEAN FORCE
under Admiral Somerville

a hit in the magazine and sank, taking with her all but three of her crew. The enemy ships turned out to be
the "Bismarck," Germany's newest battleship, and the heavy cruiser, "Prinz Eugen," both of which became
the subject of an epic chase for revenge. The picture on left, taken from the deck of H.M.S. "Prince of Wales,"
was the last ever to be taken of H.M.S. "Hood." The map on the right shows pictorially the tages of the
thrilling seventeen-hundred-mile chase which resulted, as told overleaf, in the destruction of the "Bismarck."

NAVY TAKES ITS REVENGE. After a chase lasting for nearly five days over a distance of 1,750 miles, the "Bismarck," newest and most powerful battleship of the German Navy, was sunk. During the pursuit she had been subjected to successive torpedo attacks by destroyers and aircraft of the Fleet Air Arm. These reduced her speed and enabled the battleships "King George V" and "Rodney" to establish contact on the

morning of 27 May. The gunfire of these two ships silenced her, and the Commander-in-Chief of the Home
Fleet then ordered the cruiser H.M.S. "Dorsetshire" to close in and sink her with torpedoes. At 11.1 a.m. the
battered German battleship took her last plunge. The picture, specially drawn by Frank Mason, R.I., shows the
dramatic moment as H.M.S. "Dorsetshire" launches the torpedoes that put paid to an outstanding account.

Germany's newest battleship

"BISMARCK" CHASED AND SUNK. After the sinking of H.M.S. "Hood," British cruisers maintained contact with the "Bismarck," whose speed seemed somewhat reduced. On the night of 24 May she was attacked by H.M. Aircraft-carrier "Victorious," which scored a hit, but early the next morning touch was lost. Other units joined in the chase, assisted by R.A.F. planes, and she was again located 550 miles west of Land's End on 26 May. H.M.S. "Ark Royal" attacked her twice in the afternoon, scored hits and reduced her speed; next morning,

after a 1,750-mile chase, she was engaged by battleships and sunk by a torpedo from H.M.S. "Dorsetshire," the original intention to sink her by gunfire having to be abandoned owing to poor visibility. The pictures show: left, "Bismarck" seen from a British battleship immediately before the fatal torpedo was launched; above, members of the crew of the German ship struggling in the water; about one hundred were saved by a British warship; below, "Bismarck" just after being hit by the first of H.M.S. "Dorsetshire's" torpedoes.

BITTER FIGHTING IN CRETE. On the night of 21 May the Germans endeavoured to reinforce their air-borne troops in Crete by a landing from the sea. This was intercepted by the navy which sank an Italian destroyer, two transports and a number of Greek caiques. In the picture, left, survivors of the convoy are seen being rescued by a British destroyer. In spite of this success, the Germans continued to reinforce their troops by air; by 26 May the enemy had become so strong that the British and Greek troops were compelled to retire from the Canea area, and on 28 May to the east of Suda Bay. Meanwhile Italian air-borne landings were made on the east of the island. Bitter hand-to-hand combats on land were fought by the opposing forces under continuous German dive bombing attacks from the air. The German photograph reproduced above shows Nazi troops in Crete unloading motor cycles and sidecars from a Junkers "Ju 52" transport plane.

273

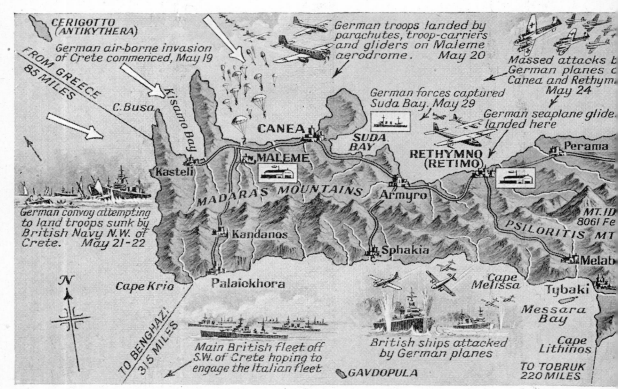

CERIGOTTO
(ANTIKYTHERA)

German air-borne invasion
of Crete commenced, May 19

German troops landed by
parachutes, troop-carriers
and gliders on Maleme
aerodrome.   May 20

Massed attacks by
German planes c
Canea and Rethym
May 24

FROM GREECE
85 MILES

C. Busa

Kisamo Bay

CANEA

German forces captured
Suda Bay. May 29

SUDA
BAY

German seaplane glide.
landed here

RETHYMNO
(RETIMO)

Perama

Kasteli

MALEME

MADARAS   MOUNTAINS

Armyro

MT. ID
8061 Fe

German convoy attempting
to land troops sunk by
British Navy N.W. of
Crete.   May 21-22

Kandanos

Sphakia

PSILORITIS   MT

Melab

N

Cape Kria

Palaiokhora

Cape
Melissa

Tybaki

Messara
Bay

TO BENGHAZI
315 MILES

Main British fleet off
S.W. of Crete hoping to
engage the Italian fleet

British ships attacked
by German planes

Cape
Lithinos

TO TOBRUK
220 MILES

GAVDOPULA

ALLIED TROOPS LEAVE CRETE. By 31 May the Germans in Crete had been so strongly reinforced from the air that further resistance by the Allies became impossible and it was decided to withdraw the troops from the island. Air power had again tipped the balance in the enemy's favour for without adequate air support the Allied troops were subject to constant bombing and were unable to obtain enough rest to keep them in good

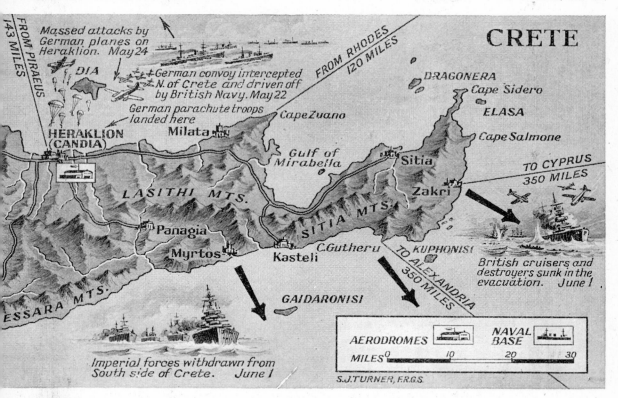

CRETE

FROM PIRAEUS 143 MILES

Massed attacks by German planes on Heraklion. May 24

German convoy intercepted N. of Crete and driven off by British Navy. May 22

German parachute troops landed here

FROM RHODES 120 MILES

DRAGONERA

Cape Sidero

ELASA

Cape Salmone

TO CYPRUS 350 MILES

Cape Zuano

HERAKLION (CANDIA)

Milata

Gulf of Mirabella

Sitia

Zakri

DIA

British cruisers and destroyers sunk in the evacuation. June 1

LASITHI MTS.

SITIA MTS.

Panagia

Myrtos

Kasteli

C. Gutheru

KUPHONISI

TO ALEXANDRIA 350 MILES

ESSARA MTS.

GAIDARONISI

Imperial forces withdrawn from South side of Crete. June 1

AERODROMES   NAVAL BASE

MILES 0   10   20   30

S. J. TURNER, F.R.G.S.

fighting condition. Evacuation began on 1 June and, in spite of violent air attacks, the Navy took off over 17,000 men for the loss of four cruisers and six destroyers. The course of the campaign is depicted pictorially in the map. The pictures show: left, an enemy dive bombing attack on shipping in Suda Bay; right, smoke rising from allied munition dumps and other war material destroyed by Royal Engineers before the evacuation.

7 JUNE, 1941. LOW-LEVEL ATTACK ON ENEMY CONVOY. In the early summer of 1941 the R.A.F. began to take the offensive, and sweeps by fighters and bombers were made almost daily over occupied France and the North Sea. In the picture above Blenheims of the Bomber Command are launching a mast-high attack on an enemy convoy off the Dutch coast. A bomb can be seen bursting close to the stern of the nearest vessel.

ALLIES CROSS SYRIAN BORDER. On 8 June British and Imperial forces under Sir Henry Maitland Wilson, co-operating with Free French troops under General Catroux, crossed from Palestine and Transjordan into Syria to prevent the Germans, with the connivance of Vichy, securing a hold on that French-mandated territory. Little resistance was encountered at the beginning of the march, which was supported by leaflet-dropping aircraft. The

British commander anxious to inflict as few casualties as possible upon Britain's former allies, ordered his troops to use force only where absolutely necessary. The pictures show: left, above, Australian infantry marching across typical Syrian country; below, shelled and burnt-out Vichy armoured vehicles abandoned by the roadside; right, Australian troops moving cautiously up a hillside during the early stages of the advance.

ALLIED PROGRESS IN SYRIA. Tyre was occupied on the second day of the march into Syria, and the general reaction of the Arabs to the Allied move was favourable, though in some quarters considerable resistance was offered, especially at Merj Ayoun, captured by Australians on 12 June. The outskirts of Sidon were reached on the 14th, and the town occupied the next day. Above, Australian troops, who distinguished themselves yet again during the advance, are seen among the ruins of the old Crusaders' castle which they have just cleared of snipers.

INFANTRY AND ARTILLERY IN ACTION IN SYRIA. After the fall of Sidon the advance along the coast continued towards Beirut. Meanwhile, in the central sector, considerable resistance was encountered which slowed down the advance towards Damascus. By 18 June, however, the encirclement of the capital was almost complete and on the following day advance forces penetrated the suburbs. The pictures show : above, British artillery in action at night, and, below, infantry taking cover behind anti-tank obstacles during their advance.

Allies enter

ALLIES OCCUPY SYRIAN CAPITAL. Free French troops approached Damascus on the 17th, and the next day were within three miles of the city. On the 19th General Wilson called on General Dentz, commander of the garrison, to withdraw his men, but the appeal was rejected and the city attacked by Free French and Indian troops, who occupied it after its evacuation on the 21st. Left, above, inhabitants watch the entry of Free French transport; below, French shells falling close to the British brigade headquarters outside the city. Right, General Catroux and General Legentilhomme (in car) drive through the city escorted by Circassian cavalry.

283

GERMANY INVADES RUSSIA

4 a.m. 22 JUNE, 1941

Suddenly and without warning the military might of Germany was hurled against Russia at dawn on 22 June, 1941. By this new act of aggression Hitler reversed the policy he initiated a year and ten months before when he signed a pact of non-aggression with the Soviet Union. That pact had itself reversed Hitler's sworn policy of the previous fifteen years, for until August, 1939, he had posed as the saviour of Europe against Bolshevism. In "Mein Kampf" he branded the Bolsheviks as "blood-stained criminals," yet in 1939 he asserted that Bolshevism was true Socialism and that the pact excluded the use of force by either side "for all eternity." In June, 1941, the Soviet Government again became the "Jewish-Bolshevist clique," and its doctrines "barbarous and vicious." The Russo-German Pact, however, did not deceive the Soviet dictator. Stalin remembered how often the perfidious Hitler had broken his solemn pledges, and during the twenty-two months between the signing of the pact and the breaking of it he strengthened the bulwarks of Russia proper by incorporating in her territory large areas on her western frontier that had passed out of her control during the war of 1914-18. Thus, when Germany invaded Poland, Russia claimed her share of the spoils, and a few months later she took territory from Finland by force after negotiations for its transfer had failed. Later Stalin acquired Bessarabia and Bukovina from Rumania, and he finally completed his protective girdle by embracing the Baltic States within the Soviet Union. Hitler's invasion of Russia was accompanied by a proclamation in which he resumed his former role of saviour of Europe against Bolshevism. "The task on the eastern front," he said, "is no longer the protection of individual countries, but the safety of Europe and the salvation of us all." Such thin pretexts deceived nobody and it was realized that Hitler's real motive was to eliminate the Red Army as a fighting force before turning upon Great Britain in a final gigantic attempt to force a decision in the west. Mr. Churchill immediately announced that Britain would give all possible aid to Russia because, he said, "any man or state who fights against Nazism will have our aid—any man or state who marches with Hitler is our foe." The pictorial representation of this world-shaking event given on this page shows the rival dictators against a background of misery and bloodshed which Hitler's latest adventure has thrust upon yet another corner of war-torn, war-weary Europe.

THE LAND HITLER SET OUT TO CONQUER. When Hitler's armies attacked Russia they embarked upon an adventure the outcome of which no one could foretell. That mighty country, covering an area of more than eight million square miles had, within a quarter of a century, developed from an almost feudal state into a highly-

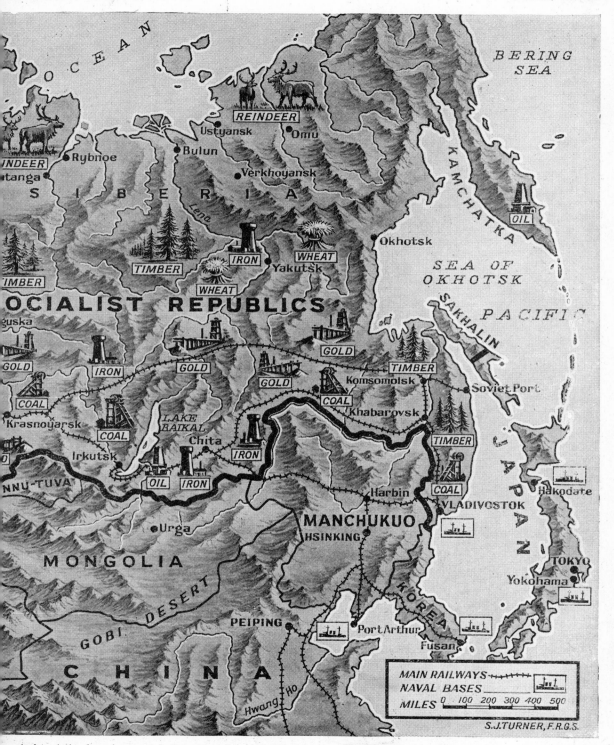

OCEAN

BERING
SEA

REINDEER

Ustyansk   Omu

Bulun

INDEER   Rybnoe

anga   Verkhoyansk

KAMCHATKA

S I B E R I A

Lena

OIL

Okhotsk

TIMBER   IRON   Yakutsk   WHEAT

SEA OF
OKHOTSK

PACIFIC

TIMBER   WHEAT

OCIALIST   REPUBLICS

SAKHALIN

guska

GOLD

IRON   GOLD   GOLD

GOLD

TIMBER   Soviet Port

COAL

Komsomolsk

Krasnoyarsk   GOLD

COAL

Khabarovsk

COAL

LAKE
BAIKAL   Chita

TIMBER

Irkutsk   IRON

COAL

Hakodate

NNU-TUVA   OIL   IRON

Harbin

VLADIVOSTOK

J
A
P
A
N

Urga

MONGOLIA

MANCHUKUO
HSINKING

TOKYO

Yokohama

GOBI   DESERT

KOREA

C H I N A

PEIPING

Port Arthur

Fusan

Hwang   Ho

MAIN RAILWAYS	
NAVAL BASES	
MILES	0 100 200 300 400 500

S.J.TURNER, F.R.G.S.

industrialized society and had built up powerful fighting services. How well these would acquit themselves
against the Nazi divisions none could tell, but the task Hitler had entrusted to his soldiers was a vast one.
The map shows the land of the Soviets together with its huge resources, which the new Napoleon set out to conquer.

NAZI HORDES ON THE MARCH. The German attack on Soviet Russia was launched along the whole of the front from the Baltic to the Black Sea, with three main drives directed, in the north through the Baltic States towards Leningrad, in the centre of Poland through Brest-Litovsk, which fell on 23 June, and in the south from Rumania through Bessarabia towards the Ukraine. On the 26th Nazi tanks made a successful break through

in the Minsk sector, but the Russians, ably supported by the Red Air Force, contested every foot of ground and inflicted enormous losses on the enemy.   The picture shows a Nazi column advancing into Russia, thrown into confusion by air attack by Russian aeroplanes.   Some of the lorries have dispersed across the fields to get clear of the road.   A well-a med bomb can be seen bursting among Nazi vehicles farther along the road.

GERMANS ADVANCE TOWARDS MOSCOW. The most successful of the German thrusts into Russia was that in the Central Sector which was directed against Moscow. Here was fought one of the greatest tank battles of the war, in which more than 4,000 tanks took part. On 26 June the enemy succeeded in breaking through the Russian defences, and four days later they claimed the capture of Minsk, capital of White Russia. The Russian plan of campaign was to allow the enemy mechanized spearheads to penetrate their lines without

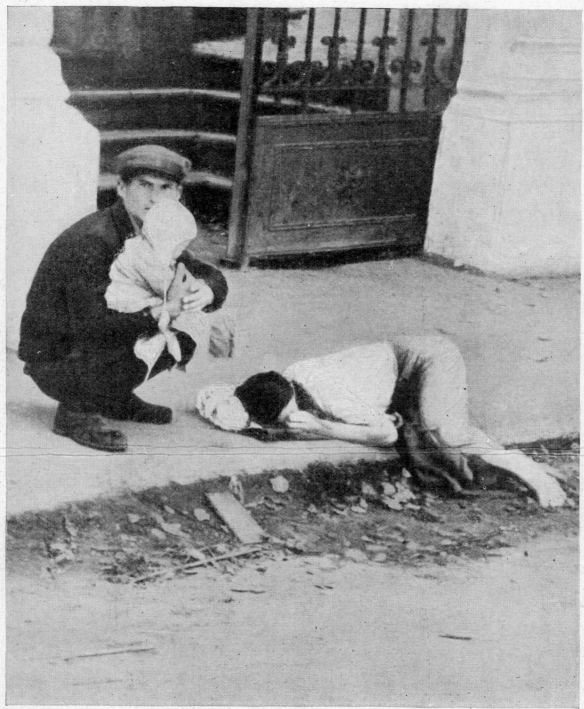

offering resistance, and then to close the gap, thereby isolating the fighting vehicles from their supporting infantry. By this means the Russians, during the first week of the war, claimed to have destroyed 2,500 tanks and to have taken more than 30,000 prisoners. The pictures show: above, left, tanks entering Minsk along a street of burnt and blown-up buildings; below, tanks in the centre of the town; right, a Russian father, fugitive from the advancing Germans, waits with his child in his arms whilst his wife lies exhausted on the pavement.

ANZACS TAKE FAMOUS DESERT CITY. Imperial and Free French troops began to close in on the ruined desert city of Palmyra on 26 June. The city, important because of its position on the oil pipe-line to Tripoli, was stubbornly defended by Vichy troops and hired Arab snipers who, however, were forced to retire, and on 3 July Allied troops marched in. Above, a Bren gun carrier is seen among the ruins of the old Roman Colonnade. The crew is hastily alighting in order to deal with any pockets of resistance that may remain.

Russian tanks hit back

RUSSIA, TOO, HAS ITS PANZER DIVISIONS. The U.S.S.R., who had for years been mechanizing its army with an eye on a possible German attack, met the onslaught of the Panzer divisions with an armoured force in no way inferior to that of the attacker. The pictures show: above, Red Army tanks moving up to the front through heavily-wooded country; they are camouflaged with branches of trees to safeguard them against observation or bombing attack by enemy aircraft; below, Russian officers of a tank column conferring at the head of their unit.

NAZI SHOCK TROOPS CROSS THE BERESINA. The Nazi drive in the Minsk sector reached the Beresina River at several points on 3 July, but it was not until several days later that the enemy effected a crossing. The picture shows German advance units preparing to force a crossing of the river by means of rafts. The blazing

buildings on the far bank have been set on fire by the retreating Russians who destroyed everything that could be of any possible use to the enemy before falling back to defence lines that had been prepared in advance. This "scorched earth" policy prevented the enemy from living on the land and taxed their lines of supply to the utmost.

SYRIA UNDER ALLIED CONTROL. Hostilities in Syria ended at midnight on 12-13 July, after a five weeks' campaign, the course of which is shown on the map. On that day General Dentz's plenipotentiaries signed at Acre the armistice terms offered them by the Free French and British commanders. These terms had been transmitted to Vichy via Washington on the 11th, but had been rejected on the grounds that it was impossible for the French Government to negotiate with the followers of General de Gaulle. General Dentz, however,

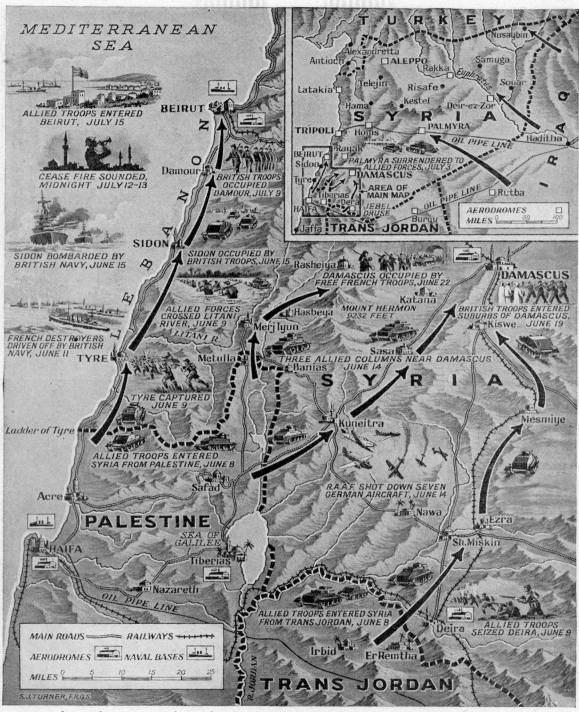

MEDITERRANEAN SEA

ALLIED TROOPS ENTERED BEIRUT, JULY 15

CEASE FIRE SOUNDED, MIDNIGHT JULY 12-13

SIDON BOMBARDED BY BRITISH NAVY, JUNE 15

FRENCH DESTROYERS DRIVEN OFF BY BRITISH NAVY, JUNE 11

BEIRUT

Damour

BRITISH TROOPS OCCUPIED DAMOUR, JULY 9

L E B A N O N

SIDON

SIDON OCCUPIED BY BRITISH TROOPS, JUNE 15

Rasheiya

ALLIED FORCES CROSSED LITANI RIVER, JUNE 9

LITANI R.

TYRE

Merj Iyun

Hasbeya

MOUNT HERMON 9232 FEET

DAMASCUS OCCUPIED BY FREE FRENCH TROOPS, JUNE 22

Katana

DAMASCUS

BRITISH TROOPS ENTERED SUBURBS OF DAMASCUS, JUNE 19

Kiswe

TYRE CAPTURED JUNE 9

Metulla

Banias

THREE ALLIED COLUMNS NEAR DAMASCUS JUNE 14

Sasa

S Y R I A

Ladder of Tyre

ALLIED TROOPS ENTERED SYRIA FROM PALESTINE, JUNE 8

Kuneitra

Mesmiye

Acre

R.A.A.F. SHOT DOWN SEVEN GERMAN AIRCRAFT, JUNE 14

Safad

PALESTINE

SEA OF GALILEE

Tiberias

Nawa

Ezra

HAIFA

Sh. Miskin

Nazareth

OIL PIPE LINE

ALLIED TROOPS ENTERED SYRIA FROM TRANS JORDAN, JUNE 8

Deira

ALLIED TROOPS SEIZED DEIRA, JUNE 9

Irbid

Er Remtha

R. JORDAN

T R A N S   J O R D A N

MAIN ROADS — RAILWAYS +++++
AERODROMES   NAVAL BASES
MILES 0 5 10 15 20 25

S.J. TURNER, F.R.G.S.

Inset map (top right)

T U R K E Y

Nusaybin

Antioch

Alexandretta

ALEPPO

Rakka

Samuga

Latakia

Telejin

Risafe

Euphrates

Souar

Hama

Kestel

Deir-ez-Zor

S Y R I A

TRIPOLI

Homs

PALMYRA

OIL PIPE LINE

Haditha

BEIRUT

Rayak

I R A Q

Sidon

PALMYRA SURRENDERED TO ALLIED FORCES, JULY 3

Tyre

DAMASCUS

AREA OF MAIN MAP

Tiberias

Dera

Rutba

HAIFA

JEBEL DRUSE

OIL PIPE LINE

Jaffa

Burqu

AERODROMES   □
MILES 0   50   100

TRANS JORDAN

---

as commander on the spot, was given a free hand to decide whether or not to continue hostilities. In the lower picture the Vichy envoy is seen leaving British forward divisional headquarters after having discussed armistice terms with the British commander. Above, General Sir Henry Maitland Wilson, with the Free French General Catroux on his right, is seen signing the treaty on behalf of Great Britain. It was estimated that during the campaign a total of between one thousand and fifteen hundred Empire troops were either killed or wounded.

W.I.P.2—K*

BRITAIN AND RUSSIA BECOME ALLIES. On 9 July, a Russian services' mission arrived in London to discuss common action to be taken against Germany by the two countries. Above, M. Maisky, Soviet Ambassador, is seen with General Golikov (in light tunic), Rear-Admiral Kharlamov (behind him, partly concealed), and other members of the mission on their arrival. Four days later Sir Stafford Cripps, British Ambassador to the U.S.S.R., in the presence of M. Stalin and M. Molotov (below) signed, on behalf of Britain, a pact of mutual assistance with the Soviet.

ONE RAID OF HUNDREDS—AND ITS EFFECTS. Representative of the continual attacks by the R.A.F. on northern France and other enemy-occupied countries was an attack in early July on Comines in daylight. Its results are visible above. The principal objective was the electric power station and direct hits were scored on the boiler house, pump house and circulating water-pipe system while several near misses caused additional damage. Direct hits were also scored on the subsidiary buildings in the area marked by a dotted line.

FIVE WEEKS OF RAIDS
BY THE R.A.F.

10 JUNE—15 JULY, 1941.

Britain's aerial offensive against Germany itself, as well as enemy-occupied countries, which had been gradually gathering momentum during the spring, entered upon a new phase of intensity on 10 June with a series of highly successful raids on Brest, St. Nazaire, Mandal and Stavanger. During the days and nights that followed, British bombers, powerfully escorted by fighters, ranged far and wide over enemy territory: almost continuous sweeps over the Channel, the North Sea and neighbouring waters, as well as over Northern France, were made during daylight and many highly successful attacks were launched on enemy shipping and aerodromes. Of the seventy-six daylight attacks made in the period under review, ten were delivered on Germany, the main targets being Bremen, Oldenburg and Kiel, where considerable damage was done to military and industrial objectives. Most of the 154 night raids were aimed at targets inside Germany, particularly in the highly important industrial area of the Ruhr. Here arms factories, railway yards, ironworks and chemical factories were attacked with the heaviest calibre bombs. During these days watchers on the British coast saw huge formations of bombers and fighters, reminiscent of the enemy formations of September, 1940, sally forth to the attack, only now they bore the red, white and blue circles of the R.A.F. instead of the black crosses of the Luftwaffe. In July the Government was able to announce that the R.A.F. had dropped within the last few weeks half the weight of bombs that the Luftwaffe had rained on British cities since the beginning of the war. The map shows the British bombers' main targets between 10 June and 15 July: white bombs indicate daylight attacks and black ones night attacks. The number of attacks on each objective is given on each bomb. In the occupied countries the appearance of the R.A.F. squadrons in "V" formation was frequently hailed with frantic cheers of welcome by the population—an extraordinary tribute to the accuracy of the British bombers' aim and the care and skill with which they confined their attentions to purely military objectives. British losses during these widespread operations were surprisingly small, amounting to 253 planes against an enemy loss of 277.

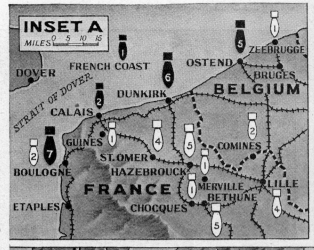

S.J.TURNER, F.R.G.S.

R.A.F. RAIDS BETWEEN JUNE 10 AND JULY 15

DAY RAIDS 3   NIGHT RAIDS 3

THE FIGURES INDICATE THE NUMBER OF RAIDS

GERMAN PLANES DESTROYED....277
BRITISH PLANES LOST........253

MILES 0 25 50 75 100

HAUGESUND
STAVANGER
NORWAY
MANDAL
KRISTIANSAND
NORWEGIAN COAST
GOTHENBURG
SWEDEN
HALMSTAD

AALBORG
RANDERS
JUTLAND
HORSENS
COPENHAGEN
MALMO

SKAGER RAK

ESBJERG
DENMARK
BALTIC

NORTH SEA

FRISIAN ISLANDS
CONVOY OFF AMELAND
NORDERNEY
TERSCHELLING
AMELAND
BORKUM
KIEL CANAL
KIEL
ROSTOCK
STETTIN

CUXHAVEN
BREMERHAVEN
WILHELMSHAVEN
EMDEN
HAMBURG

DUTCH COAST
GRONINGEN
OLDENBURG
BREMEN
BERLIN
POTSDAM

DEN HELDER
IJMUIDEN
AMSTERDAM
RHEINE
OSNABRUCK
HANOVER
MAGDEBURG

ORWICH
ROTTERDAM
HOLLAND
MUNSTER
BIELEFELD
GERMANY
HALLE
LEUNA
LEIPZIG

BELGIAN COAST
SEE INSET A
OSTEND
DUNKIRK
CALAIS
ULOGNE
ANTWERP
BRUSSELS
AACHEN
HAMM
DUISBURG
DORTMUND
KREFELD
ESSEN
DUSSELDORF
COLOGNE
SEE INSET B

DOVER
ST.OMER
LILLE
BETHUNE
BELGIUM
FRANKFURT

ABBEVILLE
MEAULTE
MANNHEIM

LE TRAIT
ROUEN

PARIS
SWEEPS OVER NORTHERN FRANCE
18
2

FRANCE

INSET B

HAMM
ESSEN
DORTMUND
SCHWERTE
DUISBURG
THE RUHR
KREFELD
MUNCHEN GLADBACH
DUSSELDORF
THE RUHR GENERALLY
RHINE
COLOGNE
AACHEN
MILES 0 5 10 15

"Blenheim" aircraft bomb

HOLLAND WELCOMES BRITISH BOMBERS. A highly successful daylight attack on Rotterdam Harbour on 16 July by "Blenheim" aircraft resulted in the putting out of action of seventeen enemy ships, totalling nearly 100,000 tons, while five other vessels were severely damaged. The planes, operating at mast-high level amid the cheers of the Dutch onlookers, also fired two large warehouses and a factory. Left, above, bursting bombs along the dockside as observed from one of the attacking planes, whose tail is seen in the left foreground; right Dutch passers-by wave greetings to the "Blenheims" from a Rotterdam suburb, a striking tribute to the bomb-aiming ability of the British airmen. Below, three of the "Blenheims" are seen flying low over the roof-tops as they "hedge-hop" their way home after the attack.

Australians enter Beirut

SYRIAN SEAPORT OCCUPIED BY ALLIES. The formal entry of the Allied troops, Australian, Indian, British and Free French, into Beirut, as provided for by the Syrian Armistice, took place on 15 July. The democratic forces received a hearty welcome from the dense crowds of inhabitants who lined the streets to cheer them (above) as their transport and guns entered the lovely city. Below are seen Australian infantry, first of the Allied forces to enter the liberated city, marching to the Place de Martyrs on the waterfront.

Empire defence measures in Malaya

EMPIRE READY IN FAR EAST. The thickening of the storm-clouds in the Far East, following on the fear of Japanese action against Indo-China and Thailand, led in July to the tightening-up of Imperial defences in Malaya, where large reinforcements of British and Indian troops and R.A.F. personnel arrived to reinforce the garrison. Above, Australian transport and Bren gun carriers crossing a Malayan bridge on manœuvres; below, men of a famous Indian infantry regiment on the march through tropical country in the peninsula.

Hot reception for the Luftwaffe July—August, 1941

GERMAN THREAT TO MOSCOW. After crossing the Beresina, the Nazis pushed on towards Smolensk, a vital junction on the railway to Moscow. Here, Russian counter-attacks brought the offensive to a standstill and inflicted huge losses on the invaders. In these operations the Luftwaffe found its match in the Red Air Force and ground defences, which together accounted for hundreds of German bombers. Above, Red A.A. guns are seen in action; the column of smoke shows that one bomber, at least will trouble them no more.

306

Attack on Knapsack power station

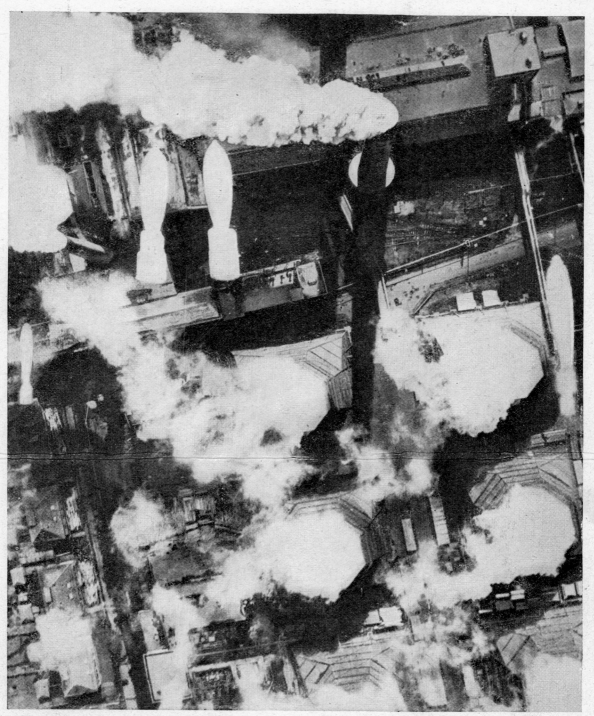

R.A.F. RAID COLOGNE IN DAYLIGHT. One of the most daring attacks of the war was made by "Blenheim" bombers of the R.A.F. when they attacked power stations at Cologne, almost at ground level, on 12 August. Many direct hits were scored in face of very heavy fire from the ground defences, and huge fires were left burning in the target area. Twelve bombers and eight fighters were lost in these operations. Above, a salvo of heavy bombs is seen falling on Knapsack power station, the largest steam power plant in Europe.

12 AUGUST, 1941. BIGGEST DAYLIGHT ATTACK OF THE WAR. Twelve squadrons of "Blenheim" bombers attacked industrial districts in Cologne on 12 August, including the great Fortuna and Knapsack power stations. Here, the attack on Knapsack is seen in full swing; on left, a "Blenheim" is circling away after having dropped its load, whilst in the distance, two more aircraft are seen dodging "flak" on their approach to the target.

RUSSIANS RETREAT TOWARDS THE DNIEPER. With their advance in the Central Sector held up, the Germans redoubled their attacks in the Ukraine. They hoped to encircle Marshal Budenny's southern army, but the Russians withdrew in good order. On the 14th they were forced to abandon Permovaisk, and two days later, after destroying the dock installations, they evacuated Nikolayev. Odessa, though encircled, still held out as the Russian armies fell back towards the Dnieper. The pictures show: top, left, motor cyclists advancing along a Ukrainian road, and, right, crossing a bridge. Below, left, horse supply wagons, and, right, tanks advancing over territory evacuated by the Russians.

CHURCHILL AND ROOSEVELT MEET

AUGUST, 1941

On 14 August Mr. C. R. Attlee, the deputy Prime Minister, gave the world by radio, particulars of a series of historic meetings between Britain's Premier and America's President which had just taken place at sea on board H.M.S. "Prince of Wales" and the U.S. cruiser "Augusta." At these meetings the statesmen of the two great democracies discussed matters of vital interest to the two countries and issued the great declaration which is reproduced below. The pictures show: above and right, the two statesmen at a Sunday morning service aboard H.M.S. "Prince of Wales" surrounded by the military and naval advisers who accompanied them; below, left, Mr. Winston Churchill hands Mr. Roosevelt a personal letter from H.M. the King.

EIGHT POINTS OF

1 Their countries seek no aggrandizement, territorial or other.

2 They desire to see no territorial changes that do not accord with the freely expressed wishes of the peoples concerned.

3 They respect right of all peoples to choose the form of government under which they will live; and they wish to see sovereign rights and self-government restored to those who have been forcibly deprived of them.

4 They will endeavour, with due respect for their existing obligations, to further enjoyment by all States, great or small, victor or vanquished, of access, on equal terms, to the trade and to the raw materials of the world which are needed for their economic prosperity.

5 They desire to bring about fullest collaboration between all nations in economic field, with the object of securing for all improved labour standards, economic advancement and social security.

6 After final destruction of Nazi tyranny, they hope to see established a peace

THE ATLANTIC CHARTER

which will afford to all nations the means of dwelling in safety within their own boundaries, and which will afford assurance that all the men in all the lands may live out their lives in freedom from fear and want.

7 Such a peace should enable all men to traverse the high seas and oceans without hindrance.

8 They believe all of the nations of the world, for realistic as well as spiritual reasons, must come to the abandonment of the use of force.

Since no future peace can be maintained if land, sea or air armaments continue to be employed by nations which threaten, or may threaten, aggression outside of their frontiers, they believe, pending establishment of a wider and permanent system of general security, that the disarmament of such nations is essential.

They will likewise aid and encourage all other practicable measures which will lighten for peace - loving peoples the crushing burden of armament.

Eastern front after eight weeks of war   22 June—17 August, 1941

GERMAN ADVANCE IN THE EAST. After eight weeks of bitter fighting the main German objectives of Moscow, Leningrad and Kiev were still in Russian hands. During the seventh and eighth weeks, however, the enemy drive in the north threatened to encircle Leningrad, whilst in the central sector, the fall of Smolensk on 13 August, brought the enemy nearer to Moscow. In the Ukraine the Russians were forced to retire towards the Dnieper, leaving Kiev at the apex of a dangerous salient. The lines of advance are shown in the map.

GERMAN THREAT TO IRAN REMOVED.

After having made several unsuccessful protests to the Iranian Government regarding the presence of an unnecessarily large German colony in that country, Britain and Russia sent troops into Iran on 25 August. Their objectives were Teheran, the capital, and the oil wells centred around Abadan (above). Only slight opposition was encountered, and on the 28th, after the fall of the pro-Nazi Government, the Shah ordered his troops to cease resisting. On 31 August, British and Russian forces met near Kazvin to the north-west of the capital, where courtesies were exchanged between the British and Russian commanders. Map shows Iran and neighbouring countries together with the lines of the advances.

NAZI PUSH IN THE UKRAINE. After the fall of Nikolayev Marshal Budenny's armies fell back in good order towards the broad River Dnieper. On 17 August, however, with the object of crossing the river higher up and outflanking the Russians, the Nazis made a determined thrust at Gomel, half-way between Smolensk and Kiev, but determined counter-attacks by "suicide divisions" held the attackers whilst the retreat farther south

continued. On 28 August the Russians announced the fall of Dnepropetrovsk, the great Ukraine steel city on the west bank of the Dnieper and the blowing up of the remaining bridges. Meanwhile the counter-attack in the Gomel area was gaining ground in spite of heavy reinforcements which the Nazis were throwing in. The picture shows German tanks in the Ukraine advancing across wheat fields that have been fired by the Russians.

MOSCOW AND LENINGRAD PREPARE THEIR DEFENCES.　While the great battle at Gomel was raging two Nazi thrusts farther north threatened Moscow and Leningrad.　The former, a continuation of the Smolensk attack, gained little ground against the stubborn Russian resistance, but the latter made more headway and on 25 August the Russians announced the evacuation of Novgorod, one hundred miles south of Leningrad. On 27 August the enemy claimed that they had cut the Moscow-Leningrad railway, and on 2 September the

Russians announced the fall of Tallinn, in Estonia. Whilst these battles were raging, the people of the two chief cities were preparing to defend their homes to the end. Women in Moscow, like those seen digging anti-tank ditches (left), worked with their menfolk to strengthen the city's defences in answer to Stalin's appeal to keep the enemy at bay at all costs. The picture on the right shows German shock troops advancing amidst the flame and smoke of burning buildings in an attempt to penetrate the flexible but unbreakable Russian lines.

319

"WE SHALL COME THROUGH"

"When I look back on the perils overcome, and on the mountain waves in which the gallant ship has driven, when I remember all that has gone wrong and remember all that has gone right, I feel sure that we have no need to fear the tempest. Let it roar, let it rage, we shall come through."

Extract from Prime Minister's Speech of 8 May, 1941

Printed in Great Britain. S. 941.